*Understandings of
the Church*

Sources of Early Christian Thought

A series of new English translations of patristic texts essential to an understanding of Christian theology

WILLIAM G. RUSCH, EDITOR

The Christological Controversy
Richard A. Norris, Jr., translator/editor

The Trinitarian Controversy
William G. Rusch, translator/editor

Theological Anthropology
J. Patout Burns, S.J., translator/editor

The Early Church and the State
Agnes Cunningham, SSCM, translator/editor

Biblical Interpretation in the Early Church
Karlfried Froehlich, translator/editor

Early Christian Spirituality
Charles Kannengiesser, editor

Understandings of the Church
E. Glenn Hinson, translator/editor

Understandings of the Church

Translated and Edited by
E. GLENN HINSON

FORTRESS PRESS
PHILADELPHIA

Library of Congress Cataloging-in-Publication Data
Understandings of the church.
 (Sources of early Christian thought)
 1. Church—History of doctrines—Early church,
ca. 30–600—Sources. I. Hinson, E. Glenn. II. Series.
BV598.U54 1986   262'.009'015   86–45227
ISBN 0–8006–1415–1

2538D86   Printed in the United States of America   1–1415

Contents

73945

Contents

Series Foreword

Christianity has always been attentive to historical fact. Its motivation and focus have been, and continue to be, the span of life of one historical individual, Jesus of Nazareth, seen to be a unique historical act of God's self-communication. The New Testament declares that this Jesus placed himself within the context of the history of the people of Israel, ushering into history a new chapter. The first followers of this Jesus and their succeeding generations saw themselves as part of this new history. Far more than a collection of teachings or a timeless philosophy, Christianity has been a movement in, and of, history, acknowledging its historical condition and not attempting to escape it.

Responsible scholarship now recognizes that Christianity has always been a more complex phenomenon than some have realized, with a variety of worship services, theological languages, and structures of organization. Christianity assumed its variegated forms on the anvil of history. There is a real sense in which history is one of the shapers of Christianity. The view that development has occurred within Christianity during its history has virtually universal acceptance. But not all historical events had an equal influence on the development of Christianity. The historical experience of the first several centuries of Christianity shaped subsequent Christianity in an extremely crucial manner. It was in this initial phase that the critical features of the Christian faith were set; a vocabulary was created, options of belief and practice were accepted or rejected. Christianity's understanding of its God and of the person of Christ, its worship life, its communal structure, its understanding of the human condition, all were largely resolved in this early period, known as the time of the church fathers or the patristic church (A.D. 100–700). Because this is the case, both those individuals who bring a faith commitment to Christianity and those interested in it as a major religious and historical phenomenon must have a special regard for what happened to the Christian faith in these pivotal centuries.

The purpose of this series is to allow an English-reading public to gain firsthand insights into these significant times for Christianity by making available in a modern, readable English the fundamental sources which chronicle how Christianity and its theology attained their normative character. Whenever possible, entire patristic writings or sections are presented. The varying points of view within the early church are given their opportunity to be heard. An introduction by the translator and editor of each volume describes the context of the documents for the reader.

Hopefully these several volumes will enable their readers to gain not only a better understanding of the early church but also an appreciation of how Christianity of the twentieth century still reflects the events, thoughts, and social conditions of this earlier history.

It has been pointed out repeatedly that the problem of doctrinal development within the church is basic to ecumenical discussion today. If this view is accepted, along with its corollary that historical study is needed, then an indispensable element of true ecumenical responsibility has to be a more extensive knowledge of patristic literature and thought. It is with that urgent concern, as well as a regard for a knowledge of the history of Christianity, that *Sources of Early Christian Thought* is published.

WILLIAM G. RUSCH

*Understandings of
the Church*

I.

Introduction

This volume contains a collection of texts illustrating early Christian understandings of the church. The plural is used advisedly because there was no single definition either within the great church or among the numerous sects on the periphery.

Selection of texts to illustrate the variety of early Christian interpretation of themselves is difficult. The first believers did not write treatises on the church in the way they wrote them on Christ or the Holy Spirit or other topics. In the vast range of early Christian literature one will find only one treatise, Cyprian's *On the Unity of the Church*, devoted more or less directly to an understanding of the church, but even there the issue is *unity* rather than *church*. The first baptismal confessions contained no article on the church, and, when one was inserted, it appeared more or less as an afterthought in connection with the article on the Holy Spirit. To be sure, the adjectives "one, holy, catholic, and apostolic" carried a lot of freight by the time they entered the Nicene-Constantinopolitan Creed, but without an understanding of the nuances which lay behind each, one will not gain much from the terms alone. Origen did not include the church among his *First Principles*, the first "systematic" theology framed by a Christian.

Dearth of direct commentary, however, is only one side, perhaps the easier side, of the selection problem. The opposite is that, while the early believers directed their energies into other projects, their understanding of the church loomed large in the background, casting its shadow in many different places. The nature of the church, for instance, figured prominently in the dialogue between Christians and Jews, the apology directed to pagans, polemic against heretics, debate with schismatics, and

1

somewhat more fraternal discussion among members of the church. Given limitations of space, however, it is impossible to reproduce complete writings or even complete sections when only a small nugget on the church lies buried within a huge mass of other material. It is always wise to give as much context as possible, but, to avoid missing some true gems, this volume includes some very brief items with a minimum of context. Although this introduction will reconstruct the setting for each selection, readers are advised to familiarize themselves with complete works.

AN OVERVIEW

The first Christian self-definitions, found in the New Testament and other early Christian writings, wrestled with the issue of Christian identity in relationship to Judaism. It could not have been otherwise. Christianity began as a sect of Judaism, and the first Christians had to interpret their existence in terms of this parentage. Some Christians, for instance, the Ebionites, never dissociated themselves from Judaism, even though they affirmed certain views which distinguished them from other Jewish sects.

As tensions mounted over Christian existence and especially their aggressive witnessing within Jewish communities, they forced a sharper self-definition. Led by the "hellenist" Stephen and the persecutor-turned-apostle Paul, Christians overcame the reluctance of "Judaizers" and decided that Gentiles did not have to become Jews by receiving the "mark" of circumcision and adhering to the ritual law in order to become Christians. According to Paul, the chief interpreter and engineer of this dramatic step, Christ has set Christians free from the law by taking them back to the pre-Mosaic covenant of God effected through Abraham. This covenant is based on faith, and by exercising the same faith as Abraham, Gentiles may enter into it. Now that Christ has come, fulfilling Jewish messianic hopes, both Jews and Gentiles must effect a relationship with God based on faith rather than on adherence to the law of Moses.

The Pauline interpretation eventually won majority support as an increasing number of Gentiles composed the churches' constituency, but it never eliminated the necessary tension which is and must remain here. The church could never have come into existence without the Jewish people, and it has drawn so many of

2

its central and essential principles from them that it can never exist without reference to them. However acrimonious the relations between parent and child, the Jewish people always confront Christians with the question put to Justin by Trypho: "If Christian piety comes from the Jewish tradition, why don't you live like Jews rather than Gentiles?"

Here is where the second phase of Christian effort to define themselves intersected. The more they succeeded in winning the Gentiles, the more they had to try to answer Trypho's query. When they attracted relatively few Gentiles, and those mostly people of modest social and economic position, they drew little comment from thoughtful pagans who could force them to articulate more precisely who they were and what they were doing. By the late second century, however, as they moved up the social ladder, they felt sharp darts from polemicists such as Celsus which provoked self-definition vis-à-vis both Judaism and paganism in its crazy quilt patterns of piety and superstition. One especially interesting response was the concept of a "third race" invented by some detractors, which Christians later turned into an argument in their favor. Yes, they were neither Jews nor Gentiles, but a people who matched and indeed surpassed the best of both.

Inevitably, incorporation of the diverse peoples of the Roman Empire and beyond generated tensions and led to divisions which would push Christian self-understanding still farther down the road. This process is clearly visible in primitive churches like that at Corinth with its Peter, Paul, Apollos, and Christ parties. By the second century the problem forced itself with powerful urgency upon churches in metropolitan centers such as Alexandria, Ephesus, and Rome, where all kinds of Christian or quasi-Christian sects—Valentinians, Basilidians, Marcionites, Marcosians, Montanists, and dozens more—competed with the church for members and influence. At this point, of course, ecclesiology blends into Christology and all other aspects of theology. The bright lights of Christianity such as Irenaeus in Lyons, Clement in Alexandria, and Tertullian in Carthage had to wrestle with definitions of the church in relationship to Judaism, paganism, and the many sects sailing under a Christian banner at one and the same time. Interestingly, as happens inevitably in times that test Christian identity, they were all forced to examine Christianity's Jewish roots more closely. A vital factor here would have been Marcion's lopping off of all ties with Judaism, but it was not the only one at work, for Christianity can never define itself without reference to its roots.

From the context of the conflicts between the churches and the sects, whether heretical or orthodox, emerged a definition captured in the formula "one, holy, catholic, and apostolic church" which has achieved a fixed place not only in Christian confessions but in the ecumenical excursions of the churches today. This formula took shape chiefly in efforts of the churches to define themselves in relation to the Montanist, Novatianist, and Donatist schisms—all three of which posed a more serious challenge because they did not deviate from the catholic church so much in vital theological principles as in matters of discipline.

Unity, of course, had been a central concern in the struggle to distinguish between orthodoxy and heresy. In making a case for their view of the matter, Irenaeus and Tertullian established the classic theory that unity (or orthodoxy) preceded diversity (or heresy). Jesus taught the disciples one system of doctrine; they founded churches and taught successors whom they appointed as bishops of these churches. Sound teaching is to be found in those same churches and in others which teach the same doctrine. The flaw in this line of argument, however, was laid wide open by Walter Bauer in his *Orthodoxy and Heresy in Earliest Christianity.* Bauer contended that diversity (or heresy) preceded unity (or orthodoxy) and that the latter was subtly imposed by force, especially by the church of Rome.

Schism heightened the issue of unity, for the Fathers recognized that the schisms, being sound in doctrine, retained a claim to be the church which heresies forfeited by unreliability in doctrine. Not surprisingly, then, Cyprian devoted an entire treatise to *The Unity of the Church* when Novatian, frustrated in his hopes of election as bishop of Rome, formed a separate sect predicated on refusal to readmit persons who secured a certificate that they had offered sacrifices required by imperial legislation as well as outright apostates. He also penned numerous letters and convened several African synods on the same theme. His insistence that persons baptized in the Novatianist church receive baptism at the hands of a Catholic bishop precipitated a near split with Rome, where Stephen required only laying on of hands, and became the foundation for the Donatist rejection of baptism by Catholics.

Holiness, although an important concept from the beginning, was raised to a higher level of visibility by the schismatics also, for all of them distinguished themselves by the rigor of their discipline. The Montanists, a charismatic sect, increased the number and severity of fasts and forbade second marriages, even if a spouse died, on the grounds that the age of the Paraclete which began with Montanus required that. In his treatise *On Purity,* Tertullian's harsh stand against forgiveness of persons guilty of numerous serious offenses epitomized the rigorist mentality shared by Montanists with Novatianists and Donatists. Novatianists rigorously opposed restoration of the lapsed to communion. The Donatists, however, took puritan logic to an extreme in the contention that toleration of *traditores* (persons who had surrendered copies of Scripture in persecution) by the Catholic Church not only endangered those persons but invalidated everything the church did—baptisms, ordinations, eucharists, etc. At issue here was whether the holiness of the church subsists in individual members or in the gifts which Christ extends corporately.

The term "catholic" was first applied to the church by Ignatius (*Smyrnaeans* 8:2) to designate orthodox Christians attached to the bishop in opposition to schismatics or heretics. In the *Martyrdom of Polycarp* (Introduction, 8.1, 19.2) it clearly denoted "universal" rather than "orthodox" (unless 16.2 is authentic). Against schismatics it could be used with force in this sense, for the Catholic Church laid claim to a larger and more universal constituency than Montanists, Novatianists, or especially the Donatists. Although Montanists and Novatianists were scattered here and there throughout the empire, the Donatists were confined to North Africa, a point on which Optatus of Mileve and Augustine hammered again and again.

Although it did not loom large in early Christian usage, "apostolic" came to prominence in authentication of the teaching of the churches. A dubious reading in the *Martyrdom* 16:2 characterized Polycarp as "an apostolic and prophetic teacher," undoubtedly meaning what Irenaeus and Tertullian would mean, that is, faithful to apostolic tradition. The term seems to have earned wider currency in the East than in the West, for it did not make its way into the so-called Apostles' Creed.

A new chapter in Christian understanding of the church opened with the conversion of Constantine. The Fathers eagerly seized the olive branch and many favors offered by the emperor. In the East especially, bishops such as Eusebius of Caesarea viewed this event as the dawn of the millennium. The church assumed a rapport with the state which, in time, would redefine its very nature and mission. In the West, already on the decline, entrenched paganism prohibited such a cosy relationship, and bishops such as Ambrose and Augustine did their best to distinguish church from empire while defending efforts of the civil realm to aid the church in its battle against competing religions. Augustine's classic distinction between the two cities—heavenly and earthly—offered a rationale for separation, even though Augustine did not equate the church with the City of God. From this time forth East and West developed their ecclesiologies along radically different lines.

THE SELECTIONS

In some ways it is unfortunate that schism and heresy exerted such a massive influence on the formation of Christian understandings of the church, for it obscured the richness of Christian reflection upon their own identity within their larger environment. Before certain lines of thinking hardened nearly everything which touched their lives, it was suggestive of their identity and calling. The earliest Christians conceived themselves, above all, as Israel under a new covenant living in the end time and called to share with the world a message of deliverance and forgiveness and reconciliation. Drawing on military parlance used by the Essenes and also widely current in the Roman Empire, they conceived themselves as the army of Christ, doing battle with the army of Satan. In baptism they renounced Satan and took an oath (*sacramentum*) to Christ. In the Eucharist they reiterated their pledge. The church itself organized in hierarchical fashion and construed its organization in military imagery despite the reservations Christians had about service in the Roman army.

An Orderly People

Clement, Bishop of Rome, interceded fraternally with the church of Corinth to restore the presbyters and deacons whom they had risen up against and expelled. Writing about A.D. 96, he reflected the still strong Jewish roots of the Roman church, citing chiefly Old Testament examples and devising an argument based on Old Testament or Jewish custom. In the passages chosen for inclusion here he sustained his pleas for orderliness by citing the examples of the army and of the Old Testament priesthood, as well as apostolic tradition.

The Gathering of a Scattered People

The *Didache* or *Teaching of the Apostles* is a church manual probably compiled for use in the churches of Syria, perhaps Antioch. Its present form dates from the early second century or, at the latest, the Montanist period (A.D. 156 or after), but it incorporates materials which are much more primitive. Selections included here, especially those which give directions for eucharists, highlight the compiler's concern for the gathering of diverse people into the one united body.

Nothing Without the Bishop

Ignatius, Bishop of Antioch, composed seven letters en route to Rome to be martyred about A.D. 110–117. In these letters he responded to the problem of divisions among the churches of Asia Minor. Although scholars have frequently envisioned a kind of Judaizing Gnosticism or Gnosticized Judaism here, modern scholarship has painted a more complex picture involving pulls in opposite directions—toward Judaism, perhaps of an Essene type, and toward Gnosticism. Ignatius's solution was to "do nothing without the bishop," a refrain repeated over and over. Frequency of repetition would indicate that episcopal authority was far from secure even in Ignatius's own see, but he was prefiguring and trying to facilitate a trend toward the monarchical episcopate.

A Secret Society

The letter in which Pliny, Governor of Bithynia, described for the Emperor Trajan the results of an inquiry he had made into Christian assemblies in A.D. 112 reveals an outsider's view of the church. In his view it was a troublesome secret society but not as evil as the popular mind imagined.

The Preexistent Church

Though associated as early as the fifth century with 1 Clement, the so-called Second Letter of *Clement to the Corinthians* appears to be an early Christian sermon composed about A.D. 140. Primarily an exhortation to good deeds and an appeal for repentance, it shows the hellenization process at work as Christianity incorporated more and more Gentiles. The depiction of Christ as male, the church as female, has a gnostic ring to it.

An Enlightened People

Justin was a pivotal figure in early Christianity's accommodation to the Greco-Roman world. Born of pagan parents in Flavia Neapolis (modern Nablus) in Palestine, he made the round of philosophies (Stoicism, Aristotelianism, Neo-Pythagoreanism, Platonism) before conversion to Christianity, in which he found what he argued was "the true philosophy." From Palestine he migrated to Ephesus and then to Rome, where he founded an evangelistic-apologetic school about A.D. 150. His students included Tatian, compiler of the harmony of the Gospels known as the *Diatessaron* and founder of the sect known as Encratites, and Irenaeus. Denounced to public authorities by a philosopher whom he had bested in a debate, he was martyred about A.D. 165.

In Justin's *First Apology*, addressed to pagans, he revealed something of his understanding of the church in a depiction of Roman baptismal and liturgical practices. Above all, the church satisfied the desire of the philosophically inclined for enlightenment. It is not surprising that Justin was the first to call baptism "the enlightenment" (*photismos*) and to argue that Christianity was "the true philosophy."

A Jewish Puzzlement

Justin also composed an apology ostensibly addressed to Judaism, but which some scholars think may have been intended for Christians unsettled in their faith by pagan use of Jewish arguments. Written in the form of a dialogue, it presents Jewish objection to Christianity and Justin's replies from the Scriptures. If this work reflects some of the internal debate over the relationship of Christianity to Judaism current at the time, as is likely, Trypho's question would have brought it all to a single focus.

Israel Under a New Covenant

In his handling of Scriptures Justin shows knowledge of rabbinic methods of interpretation, although he used mostly proof texts and "types." A great portion of the *Dialogue with Trypho* is devoted to what the church was in relation to Judaism. Curiously Justin did not elaborate on Paul's contention that the Christian covenant antedated the covenant with Moses, but he followed the lead of the author of Hebrews in claiming fulfillment of the "new covenant" promised by Jeremiah. The church is not a new Israel but the true Israel under a new covenant.

The Church of the Martyrs

The idea of martyrdom and suffering as marks of the true church was rooted in Judaism, especially Isaiah 40—55 and the Maccabean literature. Just as the earliest Christians found justification there for the crucifixion, so too did they find some basis for understanding their own vocation and *raison d'être* in a time of persecution. They attached the martyr theme to baptism, and in their worship they reiterated again and again the necessity of following in the footsteps of the Crucified One. Appeals to faithful witness to the point of death echoed over and over in time of persecution.

The eyewitness account of the *Martyrdom of Polycarp* shifted this theme into another gear. Not only did Polycarp, executed in Smyrna in A.D. 155, provide the supreme example, but his "birthday" into the eternal realm became the occasion for the gathering of the martyr church. When persecution abated, *martyria* appeared everywhere as a constant reminder of the call to faithfulness. The cult of relics sometimes veered off into degraded forms of superstition, but it also served an important function in keeping ever before the church the cost of discipleship.

Soul for the World

By the mid-second century, as Justin's writings indicate, most churches had passed the midpoint in their transition from a predominantly Jewish to a predominantly Gentile constituency. Increasing attacks by informed and educated pagans stoked the flames of reflection on the church in its relationship to the world from which it was drawing deeper and deeper draughts. Somewhere in this milieu, though the date is quite uncertain, an anonymous Christian apologist composed a defense addressed to an official named Diognetus. In it he candidly admitted that to the naked eye Christians hardly differed from other citizens of the Roman Empire. Rather, they possessed a "heavenly citizenship" alongside their earthly one that produced a dramatic difference. Whatever they might appear to be, they were to the world what the soul is to the body.

The Church as the Bank of Apostolic Truth

The struggle to arrive at some acceptable definition of orthodoxy introduced other images of the church. Prominent in Irenaeus, a seminal figure in the framing of the Catholic Church's stance, was the idea of the church as a bank into which the apostolic faith has been deposited and in which it is kept safe. A native of Smyrna, where he learned the rudiments of Christian faith at the feet of Polycarp, Irenaeus studied in Rome under Justin. From there he ventured into the wilds of Gaul. Dispatched on a mission to Rome by Bishop Pothinus he narrowly missed the massacre of Christians in Lyons and Vienne in A.D. 177. On his return he succeeded the martyred Pothinus as Bishop. About A.D. 185 to 189 he composed his massive treatise *Against Heresies*, in which he described in detail the systems of Marcion and Valentinus and gave briefer attention to the whole panoply of Gnostic teachers vying for followers during the second century.

Irenaeus knew how slippery the Gnostics could be and worked hard to construct an edifice of orthodoxy which they could not easily demolish. If he cited Scriptures, the Gnostics too would cite them, creating their own when they could not find support in those used in worship by the churches. In the end, he realized, the debate boiled down to where Christ deposited the truth he taught. He deposited it, Irenaeus insisted, in churches founded by apostles. How can one tell it has remained inviolable in them? By the list of their bishops which they can cite from the apostles on. Churches like the Roman, being the example par excellence founded not by one but by two apostles (Peter and Paul), are therefore the bank of truth.

The Church of Martyrs

The bishop of Lyons, who knew firsthand about martyrdom, gave an interesting twist to the idea that martyrs authenticate the church when he applied it to his refutation of heretics. Some Gnostic teachers counseled flight, deception, or whatever else one might do to avoid persecution. It was tricky to cite this argument, however, for the sects, notably the Montanists, also claimed martyrs and the catholic army had its own supply of defectors.

The Church as the "Born Again" Children of God

Ecclesiology has always claimed more attention in the pragmatic West than in the East, which is more mystically inclined. The mystical leanings of the East, nonetheless, have evoked understandings of the church which are in themselves beautiful and instructive. Clement of Alexandria and Origen were the major shapers of these.

Born in Athens, Clement migrated to Alexandria about A.D. 180 and attached himself to the school of Pantaenus, "the Sicilian Bee." Succeeding the latter as head of this school about A.D. 190, Clement evangelized and instructed the wave of cultured and well-educated Alexandrians now streaming into Christian assemblies. Mystical by temperament and strongly influenced by Platonism, he posited two levels of Christianity—faith and *gnosis* (knowledge). His major works reflect these levels. In an *Exhortation to the Greeks* he voiced his critique of paganism and sounded an appeal for conversion. In *The Instructor* he laid down the golden mean as the best rule of conduct for cultured converts. In his *Miscellanies*, however, he did not disguise his vexation with those who thought Christians should live on the level of faith alone, urging instead a flight to mystic realms and laying out a pattern for it.

Clement's conception of the church suited this scheme. In the *Exhortation* and *The Instructor* he spoke repeatedly of the church as the "born again" children of God. In baptism the Spirit effects the new birth. Johannine influence is obvious here.

The Church "Gnostically" Conceived

In the *Miscellanies* Clement presented his gnostic version of the church. Those who have achieved the level of perfection to which "gnostics" aspire are the true leaders of the church. Spirituality rather than ordination qualifies them for this service.

A Third Race?

The cleverest defender of early Christianity was Tertullian of Carthage. Educated in Rome perhaps in law, he was converted to the church in A.D. 195. Within a short time he composed his appeal *To the Nations*, then carefully revised it and published the revision under the title of *The Apology*. The first apologist and theologian to write in Latin, he penned a number of practical and theological treatises for use in the church of Carthage. About A.D. 206, however, attracted by its rigorous discipline, he joined the Montanist sect, which had arisen in Asia Minor about A.D. 156 or A.D. 172 (depending on which source one consults) and spread to Rome and to Carthage. In A.D. 222 he split even with them, forming a separate sect called Tertullianists. Despite his departure from the Catholic Church, his writings continued to be consulted and held in high esteem there after his death about A.D. 225 or after, testimony not only to his orthodoxy but to the acuity of his theological formulations.

In his exhortation *To the Nations*, written around A.D. 197, Tertullian gnawed on the pagan query as to whether Christians thought they were a "third race." He obviously did not like the label, but he gave later writers some ideas on using it to advantage.

A Distinctive People

Though the tag of a "third race" rubbed him the wrong way, Tertullian did not hesitate to emphasize that Christians were a "peculiar" people. In his *Apology*, a highly polished and often sarcastic defense of Christianity against paganism, he made the contrasts stand out in bas relief. Too much can be made of Tertullian's invectives, if one takes them literally, but there can be little doubt that he wanted a church which in its discipline stood out from its pagan background. Christians should "live with them but not sin with them." Dissatisfaction with the leniency of the Catholic Church doubtless pushed Tertullian toward the Montanists, who prided themselves on "more fasting than marrying," etc.

The Church of Apostolic Tradition

Tertullian employed his verbal agility and piercing wit to great effect in putting together his *Prescription for Heretics*. In this early treatise (c. A.D. 200) he repeated and elaborated on the formulas of Irenaeus. To be authentic, churches must wear the label "apostolic." Only those who hold onto and preserve the apostolic tradition have any claim to be churches.

The Montanist Church

Although Tertullian did not diverge noticeably from his position on most points of doctrine when he became a Montanist, the move brought some radical changes to his ecclesiology. There was something contradictory about this, for while he accepted the more pliant Montanist structure of the church based on inspiration and control by the Spirit, he stiffened and hardened the more tolerant and pastorally sensitive discipline of the Catholic Church. To the Montanists, of course, this represented no contradiction when viewed in terms of the ages of humankind. During the age of Law, people lived at one level. During the age of the Son, they obtained grace to do better. But when the age of the Paraclete dawned with Montanus, they had to do better still. The church is, above all, the church of the Spirit.

The Church as Superior to
All Things Pagan

Nowhere does context stand out more starkly than in claims made for the church. Speaking to their own members, the Fathers readily admitted that the church was anything but *sine macula et ruga*. Speaking to non-Christians, on the contrary, they admitted little and claimed much. The church is superior to all forms of society known by pagans, as near the human ideal as one could imagine.

This perspective was eloquently stated by Origen in his treatise *Against Celsus,* a reply to an incisive polemic composed seventy years earlier (about A.D. 178) by an otherwise unknown pagan named Celsus. With Origen Christianity reached a new plateau in its thought. Born in Alexandria to Christian parents in A.D. 185, he possessed both immense intellectual gifts and fervent piety. When the persecution under Septimus Severus claimed the life of his father, he too would have rushed out to be martyred had his mother not hidden his clothes. At age seventeen he began teaching in the school of Alexandria; at age eighteen he became its principal. He continued there until A.D. 232, when a rift with Demetrius, Bishop of Alexandria, resulted in his permanent removal to Caesarea in Palestine. Although most persons think of Origen as an Alexandrian, he composed most of his extant works at Caesarea. To Caesarea, too, he attracted bright youths such as the brothers Athenadorus and Gregory, later known as Thaumaturgus, from everywhere. Origen was arrested and tortured during the persecution under Decius (A.D. 249–251), sustaining wounds from which he never recovered fully. He died in A.D. 254.

The Double Church

Origen fills such a prominent place in early Christian theological formulation and conflict that his contributions to ecclesiology are often overlooked. Yet the eastern tradition owes a massive debt to the mystical concepts which came to classic expression in the *Celestial Hierarchies* of Pseudo-Dionysius around A.D. 500. Origen's more comprehensive thinking about this may be found in his *Commentary on the Song of Songs*, a work too complex and profuse to reproduce here even in part. The heart of his view, however, appears in nuclear form in his treatise *On Prayer*, composed shortly after he settled in Caesarea. When we worship, according to Origen, a heavenly church hovers over and around us and plugs us into the power of the Eternal. During the fourth century and after, the churches began to feature the double church in architecture and art. Observe especially the four tiers of the celestial hierarchy extending from the dome down to the basilica where the earthly church joins in.

The Church in the Bishops

How different what Cyprian dealt with in his treatise *On the Unity of the Church* and in many letters! Here is the church in its humanity, a mixed body of saints and sinners irreparably split into two or more great factions. Like others before him, of course, Cyprian had in mind the polis-church, the church of Carthage and Rome and a lot of other municipalities with their surrounding areas.

The split must have been especially grievous for Cyprian because it involved him personally at several points. A fairly well-educated lawyer converted to Christianity in A.D. 246, he rose quickly (too quickly surely) to a position of primacy in the church of Carthage, being named bishop just two years later. There was opposition to this. During the Decian persecution (A.D. 249–251), he took the advice of his clergy and went into hiding, a strategy that provoked more opposition. When persecution let up, he returned. Novatian, then a leading presbyter of the church of Rome following the martyrdom of Fabian, helped him overcome opposition to his reinstatement. When it came time for Cyprian to repay his friend, however, the story took a curious turn. In electing a successor to Fabian, Roman Christians split their vote between Novatian and Cornelius, another prominent presbyter. To resolve the stalemate, they asked the bishops of Antioch (Fabius), Alexandria (Dionysius), and Carthage (Cyprian) to help them make a decision. Fabius favored Novatian, Dionysius Cornelius. For unknown reason Cyprian delayed three months and then voted not for Novatian but for Cornelius. A disaffected deacon of Carthage named Novatus wrote to Novatian and urged him to withdraw from communion with Cornelius and Cyprian. Thence appeared the Novatianist schism in A.D. 251. The reason for the schism, according to Novatian, was not the personal factors just described but the Catholic Church's laxity of discipline, that is, its practice of restoring persons who had submitted to official demands to offer a sacrifice during the Decian persecution. Novatian did not differ in basic theological matters, being in fact the author of a widely used work *On the Trinity*, but he took a rigorist stance on forgiveness of offenders who committed serious offenses such as apostasy even under threat of persecution. Like Tertullian in his Montanist days, he admitted that God could forgive, but he refused to acknowledge that the church could forgive such sins.

In his treatise *On the Unity of the Church*, first composed in

A.D. 251 and then evidently revised during the controversy with Stephen of Rome concerning rebaptism, Cyprian made communion with the bishop the key to unity. Whoever is not with the bishop is not in the church, or, stated in another way, whoever does not own the bishop as a father cannot have the church as a mother. In the original version, which is given in the text, Cyprian posited the unity in succession from Peter as the prince of apostles and thus from the bishop of Rome. In his revised version, recorded in a footnote, he substituted a corporate interpretation. All bishops are Peter's successors.

Corpus Christianum

A new chapter in Christian self-understanding opened with the conversion of Constantine. One of the chief architects of the new understanding was Eusebius, Bishop of Caesarea and unabashed admirer of the emperor. Upon the death of Constantine in A.D. 337 Eusebius hailed him as "another Christ." History could now be schematized in a new way. Whereas before it led from Abraham to Moses to Christ, now it extended from Abraham to Christ to Constantine. Eusebius made short shrift of premillenarians. The conversion of Constantine marked the defeat of Satan and the beginning of the millennium. With the emperor lavishing favors on churches, bishops, and people, it is easy to understand why someone like Eusebius would view the church snuggling like a child in a mother's bosom into the open arms of empire, especially after the brief but severe persecution under Diocletian (A.D. 303–311). Constantine, according to Eusebius, fancied himself as "a bishop to those outside the church." He moved by stages toward that alliance between church and empire which reached its finest expression in the Byzantine Empire. No lines of separation could be drawn any longer. The cross dominated the dome of the imperial palace just as it did the dome of the church.

Corpus Permixtum

This optimistic picture of the church in relation to the empire could not depict the situation in the Latin West, where paganism remained much more firmly entrenched, despite valiant efforts to uproot it by the Emperor Constantine, some of his successors, and bishops such as Ambrose of Milan. In his concept of two cities, *civitas terrena* and *civitas Dei,* Augustine sounded a note of realism. Within the earthly city the City of God has existed from the time of Abraham, or even earlier, as a light in the midst of darkness. Although Augustine sometimes hints at connections between the church and the City of God, he always preserves some distance between the two. The City of God is the Kingdom, which does not have the limits of time, place, and sphere that the church does. The church partakes both of the earthly city and the heavenly one.

Nowhere does this stand out more clearly than in the concept of the church as a *corpus permixtum* ("mixed body") which Augustine propounded in opposition to the Donatist idea of a "pure" (*katharos*) church. Augustine, of course, entered into this controversy a century after it had begun. The Donatist schism was precipitated by a dispute over the election of Caecilian as Bishop of Carthage in A.D. 311, at the end of the persecution under Diocletian. Opponents objected to Caecilian on the grounds that he was personally unworthy and had been consecrated by a *traditor*, that is, someone who had surrendered copies of Scriptures during the persecution, and installed another in his place. Both sides appealed to Constantine. A commission sent by the emperor to investigate and then the Synod of Arles in A.D. 314 cleared Caecilian and affirmed his appointment, but this did not satisfy the opposition, which eventually took the name of a leader in the second phase, Donatus of Casae Nigrae. Fueled by African nationalism and social discontent among the original settlers, the Donatist movement competed successfully with the Catholic Church for churches and members until the Emperor Hororius issued a severe edict against it in A.D. 410. In A.D. 411 Augustine himself dealt the Donatists a severe blow at a conference in Carthage.

The Donatists raised two questions about the church and its sacraments. Does not the guilt of a minister invalidate his performance of the sacraments? Does not the Catholic Church's toleration of *traditores* in North Africa invalidate its ministry everywhere? The Donatists answered yes, Augustine no, to both questions. First, he said, the validity of sacraments does not depend on the minister but on Christ. Second, what happened in North Africa cannot possibly have corrupted the church everywhere. The church can never be "pure" in individual members. Its purity depends rather on Christ.

THE TRANSLATION

Translations are based on standard texts. Where possible, the original author's style has been preserved, so long as this could be done in acceptable modern idiom. However, cumbersome Greek or Latin sentences have been broken down to accord with modern preferences for shorter sentences. The translator has benefited from several modern, though sometimes dated, translations, but the final translations are his own and he accepts responsibility for them. Some liberties have been taken with the language to eliminate usages which might offend women. Wherever possible, generic usages of Greek *anthropos* or Latin *homo* have been rendered "person." Sometimes pronouns were replaced with nouns. Both masculine and feminine pronouns have been used to translate what in Greek or Latin was exclusively masculine when these clearly implied either. "Brothers," a favorite early Christian address, has been translated either "brothers and sisters" or "friends" when the hearers or readers would have included both. It will be evident, however, that some difficulties remain and cannot be removed without doing violence to what the writer was trying to say.

II.

An Orderly People

1 CLEMENT 37.1—38.2, 40.1—41.1, 42.1–5, 44.1–6

37.1. Let us, therefore, serve in Christ's army, brothers and sisters, with eagerness to discharge his flawless orders. 2. Let us observe how orderly, how eagerly, how obediently those who serve our generals fulfill their orders. 3. Not all are prefects nor tribunes nor centurions nor "captains of fifties" nor the rest, yet each of them fulfills the orders given by the emperor and the generals in their own rank. 4. The great ones cannot do without the little ones, nor the little ones without the great; the mixture which is in all of them is needed by all of them. 5. Let us take our body. The head is nothing without the feet, and likewise the feet are nothing without the head; the least members of our body are necessary and useful to the whole body, but to keep the whole body in working order all must coalesce and accept a single regulation.

38.1. Let our whole body be kept in working order in Christ Jesus, therefore, and let each of us be voluntarily submissive to our neighbor, just as has been established by that person's spiritual gifts. 2. Let the strong person care for the weak, and let the weak respect the strong. Let the rich person supply the needs of the poor, and the poor give thanks to God that God gave them someone to fulfill their need. Let wise persons manifest their wisdom not in words but in good deeds. Let the humble not testify in their own behalf, but leave that to others. Let those who practice continence not boast, knowing that it is another who supplies their self-control. . . .

40.1. Inasmuch as these things are evident to us and we have taken a look into the depths of divine knowledge, we ought to do in an orderly way everything which the Master commanded us to perform at the established times. 2. He commanded us to perform both sacrifices and services and that these not be done in a random or disorderly fashion, but rather at fixed times and hours. 3. He himself fixed by his supreme will both the places and the persons he wants to perform them so that everything done in a holy manner in accordance with his wishes might be acceptable to his will. 4. Those, therefore, who offer their sacrifices at the appointed times are both acceptable and blessed, for in following the laws of the Master they do not miss the mark. 5. For to the high priest have been given his own services, and to the priests has been appointed their own place, and upon the Levites have been imposed their own ministries. The lay person has been bound by orders for the laity.

41.1. Let each of us, brothers and sisters, please God in our own rank and in reverence, being in good conscience and not going beyond the rule fixed for that person's service. . . .

42.1. The apostles preached to us the good news which they received from the Lord Jesus Christ. Jesus, the Christ, was sent from God. 2. The Christ, therefore, was from God and the apostles from the Christ. Both, therefore, were sent in the order set by the will of God. 3. After they received their orders and became fully convinced by the resurrection of our Lord Jesus Christ and were entrusted with the word of God, therefore, they went out with assurance of the Holy Spirit to preach the good news that the kingdom of God was about to come. 4. Preaching from place to place and from city to city, they appointed their first converts, testing them in the Spirit, as bishops and deacons for those about to believe. 5. Now this was not new, for bishops and deacons had been written about many years before. For the Scripture says: "I will appoint their bishops in righteousness and their deacons in faith" (Isa. 60:17).

44.1. Now our apostles knew through our Lord Jesus Christ that there would be conflict over the title of bishop. 2. For this reason, therefore, having received perfect foreknowledge, they appointed those already mentioned, and afterward they laid down a rule so that, if they should die, other qualified men should succeed them in their ministry. 3. We do not think it is right, therefore, to eject from this ministry those who were appointed by the apostles or afterwards by other men chosen with the consent of the whole church and who have served Christ's flock blamelessly, humbly, peaceably, and unselfishly and who have often received accolades of all. 4. For our sin will not be small if we eject from the episcopate persons who offer sacrifices in a blameless and holy manner. 5. Blessed are those presbyters who have completed the race and who have obtained a fruitful and perfect release, for they are not afraid that anyone will remove them from the place established for them. 6. For we see that you have removed some who served well from the ministry which they have faultlessly honored.

III.

The Gathering of a Scattered People

DIDACHE 7.1–4, 9—15

7.1. Concerning Baptism, baptize as follows: Having rehearsed all these things baptize in the name of the Father and of the Son and of the Holy Spirit in running water. 2. But if you do not have running water, baptize in other water, and if you cannot baptize in cold water, do it in warm. 3. But if you have neither, pour water on the head three times in the name of the Father, Son, and Holy Spirit. 4. Before the Baptism let the person baptizing and the one being baptized and any others who can, pray, and command the person being baptized to fast for one or two days.

9.1. Concerning the Eucharist, celebrate the Eucharist as follows: 2. First concerning the cup, "We thank you, our Father, for the holy vine of David, your child, whom you made known to us through Jesus, your child. To you be glory forever." 3. Concerning the broken bread, "We thank you, our Father, for the life and knowledge which you have made known to us through Jesus, your child. To you be glory forever. 4. Just as this broken bread was scattered upon the mountains and was gathered into one loaf, so let your church be gathered from the four corners of the earth into your kingdom. For yours is the glory and the power through Jesus Christ forever." 5. But let no one eat or drink from your Eucharist except those who have been baptized in the name of the Lord. For even concerning this the Lord has said, "Do not give what is holy to the dogs" (Matt. 7:6).

10.1. But after you have eaten, give thanks as follows: 2. "We thank you, holy Father, for your holy name, which you have made to live in our hearts and for the knowledge and faith and immortality which you have made known to us through Jesus, your child. To you be glory for ever. 3. You, Master Almighty, created all things for your name's sake, and you gave human beings food and drink for their enjoyment so that they may give you thanks. But give us spiritual food and drink and eternal life through your child. 4. Above all, we thank you because you are powerful. To you be glory forever. 5. Remember, Lord, your church; deliver it from every evil and perfect it in your love, and gather it from the four winds, having been made holy, into your kingdom which you have prepared for it. For yours is the power and the glory forever. 6. Let grace come and this world pass away. Hosanna to the God of David. If anyone is holy, let that person come; if anyone is not, let that person repent. *Maran atha. Amen.*" 7. But permit prophets to celebrate the Eucharist however they wish.

11.1. Receive whoever comes and teaches you all the things mentioned earlier. 2. But if any perverted teacher teaches another doctrine so as to destroy them, don't listen to that person. But receive a teacher as the Lord if that person's teaching increases righteousness and knowledge of the Lord.

3. Concerning apostles and prophets, act according to the ordinance of the gospel as follows: 4. Let every apostle who comes to you be received as the Lord. 5. But that person is only to remain one day, and if necessary, a second. But if the person remains three, he is a false prophet. 6. When the apostle comes, he should receive nothing except bread until he finds lodging, but if he asks for money, he is a false prophet.

7. And do not test or criticize any prophet speaking in the Spirit, for every sin will be forgiven except that sin. 8. Not everyone speaking in the Spirit is a prophet unless he behaves like the Lord. The false prophet and the true prophet will be known, therefore, by their behavior. 9. A prophet who orders a meal in the Spirit does not eat from it unless he is a false prophet. 10. If any prophet does not do the truth which he teaches, he is a false prophet. 11. But no proven, true prophet, who does not teach you to do what he does, even if celebrating the cosmic mystery of the church, is to be judged by you, for he has his judgment with God, for the ancient prophets did this also. 12. Whoever says in the Spirit, "Give me money or something else," don't follow him, but if he says to give for some other person's needs, let none judge him.

12.1. Let everyone coming in the name of the Lord be

received, since you will know when you have tested that person, for you will have understanding of both right and wrong. 2. If the one coming is a traveler, help that person as much as you can, but he will not remain with you except, if need be, for two or three days. 3. If anyone who has a skill wants to settle among you, let that person work and eat. 4. But if the person has no skill, provide as you think best so that no one lives in idleness with you as a Christian. 5. But if anyone were to act like this, that person would be commercializing Christ. Beware of such persons.

13.1. But any true prophet who wants to settle among you is worthy of his food. 2. Likewise, a true teacher is as worthy of his food as is the laborer. 3. Therefore, take all the first fruits of the produce of the vineyard and the threshing floor and of oxen and sheep and give them to the prophets, for they are your high priests. 4. But if you have no prophet, give to the poor. 5. If you bake, take the first fruits and give them according to the commandment. 6. Likewise, if you open a jar of wine or olives, take the first fruits and give them to the prophets. 7. Take the first fruits of money and clothing and every possession and give them according to the commandment.

14.1. When you gather on the Lord's day of the Lord, break bread and celebrate the Eucharist, confessing your transgressions, so that your sacrifice may be pure. 2. But do not allow anyone who has a quarrel with his friend to join you until they are reconciled so that your sacrifice may not be profaned. 3. For this is what was said by the Lord: "In every place and time offer me a pure sacrifice. For I am a great king," says the Lord, "and my name is marvelous among the gentiles" (Mal. 1:11, 14).

15.1. Appoint for yourselves, therefore, bishops and deacons worthy of the Lord, men who are modest and not greedy and true and proven, for they too minister to you the ministry of the prophets and teachers. 2. So do not look down on them, for they are persons whom you have honored with the prophets and teachers.

3. Do not reprove one another in anger, but in peace, as you find in the gospel. And let no one speak or listen to anyone who has wronged another person until that person repents. 4. But do your prayers and your alms and all you do as you find in the gospel of our Lord.

IV.

Nothing Without the Bishop

IGNATIUS EPHESIANS 4.1—6.2

4.1. Whence it is fitting that you agree with the will of the bishop, as of course you do. For your very worthy presbytery, worthy of God, are in harmony with the bishop just as the strings on a harp. For this reason Jesus Christ is being sung in your concord and harmonious love. 2. Now be members of this choir, each of you, in order that being harmonious in concord and taking the pitch from God in unity, you may sing with one voice through Jesus Christ to the Father so that he may both hear and know you as members of his Son through your good deeds. It is useful, therefore, that you be in faultless unity so that you may always partake of God.

5.1. For if I in a short time achieved such fellowship with your bishop, not just human but spiritual fellowship, how much more do I consider you blessed who are united with him in this way as the church of Jesus Christ and as Jesus Christ is united with the Father so that all things may harmonize in unity. 2. Let no one be deceived: unless one is within the sanctuary, that person lacks the bread of God. For if the prayer of one or two has such strength, how much more that of the bishop and the whole church? 3. The person who does not join the common assembly, therefore, is already haughty and has separated himself. For it has been written, "God opposes the haughty" (James 4:6). Therefore, let us not oppose the bishop so that we may be subject to God.

6.1. Now as often as anyone sees the bishop being silent, let that person fear him all the more, for we must receive everyone whom the master sends to his own household just as the one sending him. It is evident, therefore, that we must look to the bishop as to the Lord himself. 2. Onesimus himself, therefore, praises highly your orderliness in God, for you all live according to truth and no heresy resides among you. On the contrary, you don't even listen to anyone unless that person speaks in truth about Jesus Christ.

IGNATIUS MAGNESIANS 6.1—7.2

6.1. . . . Strive to do everything in harmony with God, the bishop presiding in the place of God and the presbyters in the place of the council of the apostles, and the deacons, who are so sweet to me, entrusted with the ministry of Jesus Christ, who was with the Father before the world began and was manifested at the end of time. 2. All of you, then, who have received a divine agreement in your convictions, respect one another and let no one regard his neighbor in a carnal way but love one another continually in Jesus Christ. Let there be nothing among you which will be able to divide you. Rather, be united to the bishop and to those who preside over you as an example and lesson in immortality.

7.1. Just as the Lord, therefore, being united with him, did nothing apart from the Father, either by himself or by the apostles, so you do nothing apart from the bishop and the presbyters. Don't attempt to make anything look good for you by yourself, but rather let there be at the same time one prayer, one entreaty, one mind, one hope in love, in the blameless joy which is Jesus Christ, who is unsurpassable. 2. All of you hurry together as to one temple of God, one altar, one Jesus Christ, who came forth from one Father and is with one and has departed to one.

IGNATIUS SMYRNAEANS 7.1—9.1

7.1. The heretics stay away from the Eucharist and prayer because they do not confess that the Eucharist is the flesh of our Savior Jesus Christ which suffered for our sins and which the Father raised up in his kindness. Those who deny the free gift of God, therefore, die in disputes. It would be better for them to love so that they may share in the resurrection. 2. It is good to stay away from such persons and not even to talk about them either in private or in public but to pay attention to the prophets and especially to the Gospel in which the passion has been manifested to us and the resurrection has been completed. But flee divisions as the worst of evils.

8.1. All of you follow the bishop as Jesus Christ follows the Father and the presbytery as if it were the apostles. But respect the deacons as God's command. Let no one do any of the things decreed for the church without the bishop. Let that be counted a valid Eucharist which is celebrated by the bishop or by someone he authorizes. 2. Wherever the bishop appears, there let the meeting be, just as wherever Jesus Christ is, there is the catholic church. It is not permitted either to baptize or to hold the *agape* without the bishop, but whatever he approves is acceptable also to God so that whatever you do may be safe and valid.

9.1. Finally, it is good that we be serious since we still have time to repent toward God. It is good to know God and the bishop. A person who honors the bishop has been honored by God. One who does anything without the bishop's knowledge serves the devil. . . .

V.

A Secret Society

LETTER OF PLINY TO THE
EMPEROR TRAJAN 7

But [the accused Christians] declared that the sum of their guilt or error had amounted only to this, that on an appointed day they had been accustomed to meet before daybreak, and to recite a hymn antiphonally to Christ, as to a god, and to bind themselves by an oath, not for the commission of any crime but to abstain from theft, robbery, adultery, and breach of faith, and not to deny a deposit when it was claimed. After the conclusion of this cere-mony it was their custom to depart and meet again to take food; but it was ordinary and harmless food, and they had ceased this practice after my edict in which, in accordance with your orders, I had forbidden secret societies.

VI.

The Preexistent Church

2 CLEMENT 14.1–5

And so, brothers and sisters, if we do the will of our Father, God, we will be a part of the first church, the spiritual one, which was created before sun and moon. But if we will not do the will of the Lord, we will be like the Scripture says, "My house has become a den of thieves" (Jer. 7:11). Therefore, let us choose to be a part of the church of life in order that we may be saved. 2. I do not suppose that you are unaware that the living church is the body of Christ, for the Scripture says, "God made humankind male and female" (Gen. 1:27). The male is Christ, the female is the church. And yet the books and the apostles do not say that the church is present, but rather they say it is from above. For she was spiritual, just as our Jesus is also, and she was manifested in the last days that she may save us. 3. Now the church, being spiritual, was manifested in the flesh of Christ, making clear to us that if any of us guard her in the flesh and do not corrupt her, they shall receive her back again in the Holy Spirit, for the flesh is the antitype of the Spirit. No one, therefore, who corrupts the antitype will receive the real thing. This means, then, brothers and sisters, guard the flesh in order that you may partake of the Spirit. 4. Now if we say that the flesh is the church and the spirit is Christ, then the one who mistreats the flesh mistreats the church. Such a person, therefore, will not partake of the Spirit, which is Christ. 5. This flesh is capable of sharing in such life and immortality when the Holy Spirit is united with it, and no one can express or talk about what the Lord has prepared for his elect.

VII.

An Enlightened People

JUSTIN 1 APOLOGY 61, 65—67

61. I will explain also the manner in which we have committed ourselves to God when we have been renewed through Christ lest we seem to do some harm by leaving something out. As many persons as are persuaded and believe that what we have taught and said is true and promise that they can live in this way, they are instructed to pray and, fasting, to ask God to forgive the sins they have committed, while we pray and fast together with them. Then they are brought by us to a place where there is water and are reborn in the same way in which we ourselves have been reborn. For they then receive the water bath in the name of God, the Father and Master of the universe, and our Savior Jesus Christ and the Holy Spirit. For Christ himself said, "Unless you are born again, you cannot enter the kingdom of heaven" (John 3:5). Now everybody knows that those who have been born once cannot enter their mothers' wombs again. And it has been declared by Isaiah, the prophet, as I wrote earlier, how those who have sinned and repent should flee their sins. He said: "Wash. Be clean. Take away the evils from your souls. Learn to do good. Be fair to the orphan and defend the widow. And come, and let us reason together, says the Lord. Although your sins are as scarlet, I will make them white like wool; although they are as crimson, I will make them white like snow. But if you do not listen to me, a sword will devour you, for the mouth of the Lord has spoken it" (Isa. 1:16–20).

Now we have learned the reason for this rite from the apostles. Since we have been born of necessity, ignorant of our first birth, by the sexual union of our parents with one another and have been reared with bad habits and evil training; so that we may not remain children of necessity or ignorance but may obtain forgiveness of the sins we have already committed, the name of God, the Father and Master of the universe, is named in the water over the person who wants to be born again and has repented for the sins committed. This name alone is pronounced at the laver by the one who leads this person there. For no one has a name to call the unnameable God; and if anyone should dare to say God has a name, that person is insane. The one being enlightened is washed also in the name of Jesus Christ, crucified under Pontius Pilate, and in the name of the Holy Spirit, who spoke through the prophets and proclaimed beforehand everything about Jesus.

65. After we have washed in this way the person who has been persuaded and has given assent, we lead that one to the place where those called brothers and sisters are gathered, praying vigorously for themselves and for the person being illumined and for all others everywhere, so that, learning the truth, we may also be counted worthy to be found good citizens and keepers of the commandments in order to obtain eternal salvation. When we have stopped praying, we greet one another with a kiss. Then bread and a cup of wine mixed with water are brought to the person presiding. Taking them, he sends up praise and glory to the Father of the universe through the name of the Son and the Holy Spirit and gives thanks at length for being counted worthy of these things by God. When he has completed the prayers and thanksgiving, all the people present assent, "Amen." "Amen" in Hebrew means "so be it!" When the one presiding has given thanks and all the people have assented, those we call deacons allow each of the persons present to partake of the bread and the wine mixed with water over which the thanksgiving has been pronounced and they take some to those not present.

66. Now we call this food the thanksgiving (eucharist). No one is permitted to partake of it except one who believes that what we have taught is true and who has been washed in the laver for forgiveness of sins and for rebirth and who lives in the way Christ instructed. For we do not receive these like plain bread or plain drink; rather, as Jesus Christ, our Savior, who became incarnate through the Word of God, had both flesh and blood for our salvation, so also have we been taught that the food, over which

thanks have been spoken through the prayer of his very own word and by which our flesh and blood are nourished by transmutation, is the flesh and blood of that Jesus who became incarnate. For the apostles, in their memoirs which are called "Gospels," have passed on what was commanded of them: that Jesus, taking bread, having given thanks, said, "Do this in remembrance of me, this is my body" (Luke 22:19); and likewise taking the cup and giving thanks, said, "This is my blood"; and gave it to them alone. Evil demons have also passed this on in the mysteries of Mithra, commanding it to be done, for you know or else can learn that bread and a cup of water are put in the mystic rites of the one being initiated with certain incantations.

67. Afterward we continually remind one another of these things. And we who are affluent help all the needy, and we are always together. For all we bring we bless the Maker of all things through his Son, Jesus Christ, and through the Holy Spirit. Now on the day called Sunday there is a meeting of all those who live in cities or in the country, and the memoirs of the apostles or the writings of the prophets are read as long as time allows. Then, when the reading has stopped, the person presiding gives verbal instructions and challenges the imitation of good things. Then we all stand up together and send up prayers. Then, as I said before, when we have stopped praying, bread and wine mixed with water are brought, and the person presiding sends up prayers and thanksgivings, insofar as he is able, and the people assent, saying, "Amen!" Then there is a distribution and reception of the elements to each, and what is left is taken by the deacons to those not present. Persons who are well to do and wish to do so each give whatever they choose, and the collection is distributed by the person presiding. He takes care of orphans and widows and those in need on account of sickness or for some other reason and those who are in prisons and aliens who are passing through and, in a word, all those who are in need. But we all meet together on Sunday, since it is the first day, on which God made the world, transforming darkness and matter, and since Jesus Christ, our Savior, was raised from the dead on that day. For they crucified him the day before Saturday, and on the day after Saturday he appeared to his apostles and disciples and taught these things which have been submitted also to you for examination.

VIII.

A Jewish Puzzlement

TRYPHO IN JUSTIN
DIALOGUE WITH TRYPHO 10

This is what perplexes us most: that you, though claiming to be religious and thinking you are better than others, do not separate yourselves from the Gentiles in any respect and do not differ from them in your manner of life—either in keeping feast days and sabbaths or in having circumcision. Instead, you put your hopes in a crucified man and thus hope to obtain something good from God even though you do not do his commandments.

IX.

Israel Under a New Covenant

JUSTIN *DIALOGUE* 119—120

119. . . . For this is that people which God promised to Abraham long ago, and he promised to make him the father of many peoples, not meaning Arabs or Egyptians or Idumeans, since Israel also became the father of a great people, and Esau as well; and there is now a great number of Ammonites. Noah also was the father of Abraham, and indeed of the whole human race; but others were the forbears of other people. What more, then, did Christ grant to Abraham? That he called him with his own voice through the same calling, telling him to depart from the land in which he was living, and he called us all through that same voice, and we have already departed from the country in which we lived according to the evil standards of other citizens of the earth. With Abraham we will inherit the holy land, receiving the inheritance of an unfading eternity, being children of Abraham on account of the same faith. For just as he believed the voice of God and it was "accounted to him for righteousness," so also we have believed the voice of God which has been spoken through the apostles of Christ and again was preached through the prophets, and have renounced all things in the world until we die. He promises to Abraham, therefore, a people of like faith—reverent and righteous and pleasing to the Father, but it is not you, "In whom there is no faith" (Deut. 32:20).

120. You see how God promises these same things to both Isaac and Jacob: "And all the nations of the earth will be blessed in your seed" (Gen. 26:4). And to Jacob, "And all the tribes of the earth shall be blessed in you and in your seed" (Gen. 28:14). He no longer says this to Esau or Reuben or any other, but rather to

34

those from whom the Christ was about to come according to the dispensation which was arranged through the Virgin Mary. But if you would consider the blessing of Judah, you would understand what I mean. For the seed is divided from Jacob and comes down through Judah and Phares and Jesse and David. Now this was a sign that some of your people would be children of Abraham, being found also in the portion of Christ, but others are also children of Abraham, since they are as the sand on the seashore, which is impotent and fruitless, being numerous and uncountable, but bearing no fruit at all but only drinking the seawater. A multitude of your people is reproved for this reason, drinking bitter and godless doctrines but spitting out the Word of God. He speaks also, therefore, in a statement relating to Judah: "No prince shall be lacking from Judah or leader from his thighs until what has been decreed for him occurs; and he will be what the people are waiting for" (Gen. 49.10). Now it is clear that this was not spoken about Judah but about Christ. For not all of us from all the nations are waiting for Judah, but rather for Jesus, who also led your fathers out of Egypt. For until the coming of Christ the prophecy proclaimed, "Until the one who is appointed comes, he too will be what the people are waiting for." He came, therefore, as I have shown in many ways, and Jesus is expected to come again upon the clouds, he whose name you profane and work to have profaned all over the earth.

X.

The Church of the Martyrs

MARTYRDOM OF POLYCARP 16.2—18.3

16.2. One of these elect was indeed the most wonderful martyr Polycarp, who was in our own times an apostolic and prophetic teacher, Bishop of the Catholic Church in Smyrna. For every word he spoke was both fulfilled and will be fulfilled.

17.1. But the jealous and envious and evil one who is the adversary of the righteous type, seeing the greatness of his witness and his blameless conduct from the beginning, and that he had been crowned with an incorruptible crown and had carried off the incontestable prize, took care that we not carry away even his physical remains, although many of us wanted to do this and to have communion with his holy flesh. 2. Therefore, he sent Nicetas, the father of Herod and the brother of Alce, to ask the governor not to give his body to us, "lest," he said, "forsaking the crucified one, they begin to worship this person." Now they said this because the Jews, who watched when we were about to take his body from the fire, instigated and urged them. They do not know that we will never be able to forsake Christ, who suffered for the salvation of those being saved throughout the world, an innocent person suffering for sinners, nor to worship any other. 3. For we worship him as the Son of God, but we rightly love the martyrs as disciples and imitators of the Lord because of their flawless commitment to their own King and Teacher. Would that we might be both their comrades and their fellow-disciples.

18.1. When the centurion saw the contentiousness inspired by the Jews, he put the body in their midst, as their custom was, and burned it. 2. And so we later picked up his bones, more precious than costly stones and purer than gold, and put them in a suitable place. 3. There the Lord will permit us to gather when possible in gladness and joy to celebrate the "birthday" of his martyrdom, both for remembrance of those who have already waged their contest and for training and preparation of those about to do so.

XI.

Soul for the World

EPISTLE TO DIOGNETUS 5.1—6.10

5.1. For Christians have been distinguished from other persons neither by country nor by language nor by customs. 2. For nowhere do they dwell in cities of their own, nor do they use any strange dialect, nor do they strive for a peculiar lifestyle. 3. This teaching of theirs has not been discovered by some intellect and thought of the curious, nor are they proponents of human dogma as some are. 4. Rather, while dwelling in both Greek and barbarian cities, according to the lot which has fallen to each, and following local customs as regards clothing and food and the rest of life, they display the marvelous and admittedly strange character of their own citizenship. 5. They live in their own countries, but as aliens. They participate in everything as citizens, but they endure everything as strangers. Every foreign country is their fatherland, and every fatherland a foreign country. 6. They marry just like all persons do and they beget children, but they do not discard unwanted children. 7. They set a common table, but they are not promiscuous. 8. They live out their lot "in the flesh," but they do not live "according to the flesh." 9. They spend their time on earth, but they have their citizenship in heaven. 10. They obey the established laws, but they surpass the laws in their own lives. 11. They love all persons, and yet they are persecuted by all. 12. They are unknown, and yet they are condemned; they are put to death, and yet they come back to life. 13. They are poor, and yet they enrich many; they lack everything, and yet they have plenty of everything. 14. They are dishonored, and yet they are praised in the dishonors. They are blasphemed, and yet they are justified. 15. They are reviled, and yet they are blessed; they are insulted, and yet they honor others. 16. Though they do good, they are punished as evildoers; though they are punished, they rejoice as those who come back to life. 17. They are fought by Jews as foreigners and persecuted by Greeks; and those who hate them cannot give the reason for their enmity.

6.1. To say it simply, what a soul is in a body, that is what Christians are in the world. 2. The soul is spread through all the members of the body, and Christians throughout all the cities of the world. 3. A soul dwells in the body, but it is not "of the body"; and Christians dwell in the world, but they are not "of the world." 4. The soul, though invisible, is guarded in the visible world, but their devotion remains invisible. 5. The flesh hates the soul and wages war against it, but it does it no harm, because it is hindered for indulging in its pleasures; and the world hates Christians, but it can do them no harm, because they resist its pleasures. 6. The soul loves the flesh, which hates it, and also the limbs; and Christians love those who hate them. 7. The soul has been confined to the body, but it itself sustains the body; and Christians are confined in the world as in a prison, but they themselves sustain the world. 8. The soul dwells immortal in a mortal tent; and Christians dwell in corruptible things awaiting incorruption in heaven. 9. When badly treated as to food and drink, the soul does better; and when buffeted day by day, Christians increase still more. 10. God has appointed them for such a commission which it is not right for them to refuse.

XII.

The Church as the Bank of Apostolic Truth

IRENAEUS *AGAINST HERESIES* 3.3.1, 3.4.1–2, 3.24.1, 4.26.2

3.3.1. So it is within reach of all who want to see the truth to discern the tradition of the apostles which has been manifested in the whole world. All we have to do is to list those who are appointed bishops in the churches by the apostles and their successors up to our own time who neither taught nor recognized anything like that which the heretics rave about. For even if the apostles would have known "secret mysteries" which they used to teach the "perfect" separately and secretly apart from the others, they would especially have passed these things down to those to whom they also were entrusting the churches themselves. For they wanted those whom they left as successors to be quite perfect and beyond reproach in all things, handing over to them their own place as teachers. To those who do what is right this would have great usefulness, but to those who fall away it would be a great disaster. But since it would take too long in a volume such as this to list the successions of all the churches, we will indicate only those of the greatest and most ancient church of Rome, recognized by all and founded and established by the two most glorious apostles, Peter and Paul. This church has the tradition handed down to us through successions of bishops. In this way we throw into confusion all who, in whatever way, gather in unauthorized meetings by reason of self-serving evil or vainglory or blindness and evil thought. For it is necessary that every church, that is, persons who are faithful everywhere to the tradition which has been handed down from the apostles which has been conserved by those who are everywhere, agree with this church on account of its more powerful origin [with these two apostles].

3.4.1. Since there are such proofs, therefore, it is not appropriate to seek among others the truth which it is easy to obtain from the church, for the apostles conferred fully on her all that there is of the truth, like the rich deposit money in banks, so that whoever wants may obtain the water of life from her. For she is the doorway to life; but all others are thieves and robbers. For this reason it is necessary certainly to avoid *them*, but to choose with the highest care what is of the church and to lay hold on the tradition of truth. Why? Should there be a dispute about some ordinary question, would it not be necessary to have recourse to the most ancient churches to which apostles came and to obtain from them what is certain and clear about the present question? But what if the apostles had not left us any writings? Would it not be necessary to follow the order of tradition which they passed on to those to whom they entrusted churches? To this arrangement many of the barbarian peoples who believe in Christ assent, having salvation written in their hearts without paper or ink and diligently keeping the ancient tradition, believing in one God, Maker of heaven and earth and everything that is in them through Christ Jesus, God's Son. On account of his most exalted love toward his creation, he underwent that birth which was from a Virgin, uniting humankind with God through himself, suffered under Pontius Pilate, and rising again was taken up in splendor and is about to come in glory as the Savior of those who are to be saved and judge of those who are to be judged and sent into eternal fire as the transformers of truth and despisers of his Father and his coming. Those who have believed this faith as a result only of our spoken word because they are illiterate are barbarians, but as regard their thought, manner, and behavior, they are exceedingly wise on account of faith, and they please God, living in full justice and chastity and wisdom. If anyone should proclaim to them what is invented by the heretics, speaking in their own language, they would immediately stop up their ears and flee as far as they could, not bearing to listen to some blasphemous speech. Thus through that ancient tradition of the apostles they admit into their thinking none of the portentious speech of the heretics, for the latter neither had a congregation among them nor established any doctrine.

3.24.1. . . . But we have shown how the preaching of the church is consistent everywhere and persists equally and has behind it the testimony of the prophets and the apostles and all the disciples through the beginning, middle, and end and through the whole saving plan (*oikonomia*) of God and that solid system which is in our faith which lends itself to human salvation. We keep what we have received from the church and what is always from the Spirit of God like some precious deposit growing in a good vase which also makes the vase it is in to grow. For this gift of God has been entrusted to the church, like the breath of creation, so that all the members receiving it may be made alive. And in it has been deposited the means of communicating with Christ, that is, the Holy Spirit, the earnest of incorruption and confirmation of our faith and ladder of ascent to God. "For in the church," [Scripture] says, "God has appointed apostles, prophets, teachers" (1 Cor. 12:28), and all the other working of the Spirit. All who do not gather with the church but defraud themselves of life through evil thought and worse deed do not participate in the Spirit. For where the church is, there is the Spirit of God; and where the Spirit of God is, there is the church and every gift; and the Spirit is truth. Accordingly, those who do not participate in the Spirit are not nourished unto life by the mother's breasts nor do they receive that brilliant fountain which flows from the Body of Christ. Rather, they dig for themselves broken cisterns in dirty ditches and they drink putrid water from the dirt, fleeing the faith of the church, lest they be convicted, rejecting the Spirit that they may not be instructed.

4.26.2. Wherefore it is necessary to obey those who are presbyters in the church, those who hold the succession from the apostles, just as we have proven, who have received a definite gift of the truth together with the succession of the episcopate according to the pleasure of the Father. But it is necessary also to be suspicious of others who depart from the primitive succession and gather in any place whatever, [regarding them] either as heretics with evil intention or as schismatics who are inflated with pride and self-centered, or again as hypocrites, doing this for the sake of money and vainglory. But all these have fallen from the truth. And heretics who offer strange fire at the altar of God, that is, alien teachings, will be burned by heavenly fire, like Nadab and Abihu (Lev. 10:1-2). But those who rebel against the truth and encourage others against the church of God will remain among those in hell, swallowed up by an earthquake, like Korah, Dathan, and Abiram (Num. 16:33). But those who split and divide the unity of the church will receive from God the same punishment as Jeroboam (1 Kings 14:10).

XIII.

The Church of Martyrs

IRENAEUS *AGAINST HERESIES* 4.53.1–55.1

4.53.1. He will also judge those who cause schisms, who are empty of the love of God and look out for their own advantage rather than the unity of the church, and who, for little reasons, or any other kind, cut and divide the great and glorious body of Christ and, insofar as they can, kill it; who talk peace and wage war, truly "straining at the gnat and swallowing the camel" (Matt. 23:24). There can be no reformation great enough to compensate for the harm caused by their schism. He will judge also all those who are outside the truth, that is, who are outside the church, but he will himself be judged by no one. For all things are consistent to him. He has a complete faith in one God, the Almighty, from whom everything; and he has a sure commitment to the Son of God, Jesus Christ, our Lord, through whom everything, and his dispensations, through which the Son of God became human; and to the Spirit of God, who leads to a knowledge of the truth and explains the dispensations of the Father and the Son according to which he dwelt among human beings in each generation, just as the Father wishes.

2. True knowledge consists of the teaching of the apostles, and the ancient constitution of the church throughout the world, and the stamp of the body of Christ according to the successions of bishops to whom [the apostles] handed on that church which exists in every place, which has come down to us. In the church is found the most complete handling of truth (*tractatio*) conserved without any fabrication of Scriptures. She receives truth without adding to it or subtracting from it. There is reading without falsification, and legitimate and careful explanation in line with the Scriptures, both without danger and without blasphemy. [True

44

knowledge consists] especially of the gift of love, which is more precious than knowledge, more glorious than prophecy, excelling all the other spiritual gifts.

4.54. Accordingly, the church everywhere sends forth a multitude of martyrs all the time because of the love which she has toward God. But all the others not only do not have those who demonstrate this thing among themselves, but they even say that such witness is not necessary, for their true witness is what they think. The only exception is that one or two now and then in the whole period since the Lord appeared have borne reproach for the name at the same time with our martyrs (as if that person also obtained mercy) and was led with them like some kind of retinue given to them. For the church alone purely sustains the reproach of those who suffer persecution for righteousness' sake and endure all the punishments and are put to death because of their love for God and confession of His Son. Often she is weakened and yet immediately increases her members and gets well, just like her type, Lot's wife, who became a pillar of salt. She is also like the ancient prophets who endured persecution, as the Lord says, "For so did they persecute the prophets who were before you" (Matt. 5:12), for she suffers persecution anew certainly at the hands of those who do not receive the Word of God while the same Spirit rests upon her. Now the prophets indeed prophesied along with the other things which they were prophesying that whomever the Spirit of God rested upon and were obedient to the Word of the Father and served him as they could would suffer persecution and be stoned and be killed. For in themselves the prophets were prefiguring all these things because of their love of God and because of his Word.

4.55.1. For since they were themselves members of Christ, each one of them disclosed his prophecy according to that member he represented, all of them, though many, prefiguring and declaring things which pertain to one person. For as the working of the whole body is displayed by our members, but the form of the whole person is not displayed by *one* member, but rather by *all*, so also all the prophets were indeed prefiguring one person, but each of them fulfilled his place according to the member he represented and thus prefigured the work of Christ represented by that member.

XIV.

The Church as the "Born Again" Children of God

CLEMENT OF ALEXANDRIA
EXHORTATION TO THE GREEKS
4.59.2–3; 9.82.4–7, 88. 2–3

4.59.2 We have become an offering consecrated to God on behalf of Christ. "We are the chosen race, the royal priesthood, a holy nation, a peculiar people, who once were not a people but now are the people of God" (1 Pet. 2:9–10). As John says, we are not those who are "from below" but rather those who have learned everything from the One who came from above, who have come to understand the saving plan (*oikonomia*) of God, who have learned to walk "in newness of life" (Rom. 6:4).

9.82.4. Come! Come! O my young people. "For if you do not become like little children and be born again," as the Scripture says, you may not receive the Father who truly is, "nor will you ever enter into the kingdom of heaven" (John 3:5; Matt. 18:3). For how is the stranger permitted to enter? Only, I think, when one is enrolled and becomes a citizen and receives the Father will that person be "among those of the Father" (Luke 2:49), be counted worthy to share in the inheritance and participate in the Father's kingdom with his true Son, the "beloved" (cf. Matt. 3:17; Mark 1:11; Luke 3:22; John 1:34). For this is the first born church which is composed of many good children, that is, the "first born whose names are inscribed in heaven" and who celebrate worship with such "myriads of angels" (cf. Heb. 12:22–23). But we too are first born children, we who are reared by God, the genuine friends of the "first born," the first of other persons who have come to know God, the first who have been pulled free from sins, the first who have been separated from the Devil. . . .

9.88.2. Let us hasten to salvation, to regeneration. Let us who are many hasten to be gathered into the one love according to the unity of the monadic Being. As we are made good, let us strive for unity in the same way, seeking the good Monad. Now the union of many, taking on a divine harmony from multiple notes and differences, becomes a divine symphony, when it follows one choir director and teacher, the Word, and rests upon the same truth, saying, "Abba, Father" (Mark 14:36; Rom. 8:15). God welcomes this sound as the one which is truly from his own children and receives from them their first fruits.

CLEMENT OF ALEXANDRIA *THE INSTRUCTOR*
1.6.26.1, 1.6.30.1–31.2, 1.6.42.1–43.1

1.6.26.1. This same thing also happens concerning us, whose model the Lord became. Being baptized, we are illuminated. Being illuminated, we are adopted as children. Adopted as children, we are perfected. Perfected, we become immortal. "I said," the Scripture says, "you are all gods and children of the Most High" (Ps. 82:6). Now this work is variously called "spiritual gift" and "illumination" and "perfection" and "washing." It is the "washing" by which we are cleansed of our sins. It is the "spiritual gift" by which the penalty for sins is removed. It is the "illumination" by which that holy light which saves is perceived, that is, by which we get a clear vision of the divine. "Perfection" we say is that which lacks nothing. For what does one who knows God lack? For how truly out of place to call what is incomplete a "spiritual gift" of God, when, being perfect, he surely gives perfect gifts. As everything came into existence at his command, so when he merely wishes that grace be given it is fulfilled. For what is about to happen in time is anticipated by the power of his will.

30.1. We are cleansed, therefore, of all our sins, and we are no longer shackled by evil. This single gift of illumination means that we are no longer like we were before we were washed. Because knowledge rises like the sun with the illumination, streaming through the mind, we who were untaught, before the instruction is given, immediately hear as disciples, for you could not tell when it happened. 2. For the catechesis leads to faith, but faith together with holy Baptism is guided by the Spirit. That faith involves the universal salvation of humankind and is given equally and in common to all persons by the righteous and loving God, the apostle has then explained quite clearly: 3. "Now before faith came, we were guarded under law, confined for the faith about to be revealed. So the Law was our pedagogue to Christ in order that we might be justified by faith. But now that faith has come, we are no longer under a pedagogue" (Gal. 3:23–25). 31.1. Do you not hear that we are no longer under that law which was accompanied by fear, but under the Word, the Instructor in free will? Then the apostle added the note that this is without partiality. "For you are all children of God through faith in Christ Jesus. For as many of you have been baptized into Christ, you have put on Christ. There is no longer Jew nor Greek, slave nor free, male nor female, for you are all one in Christ Jesus" (Gal. 3:26–28). 2. There are therefore not two classes in this Word— gnostics and psychics, but all who have laid aside carnal desires are equally spiritual before the Lord. And he writes again elsewhere, "For we have all been baptized into one body, whether Jews or Greeks, slaves or free persons; and all of us drank one drink" (1 Cor. 12:13).

42.1. O mystic marvel! One is the universal Father, and one too is the universal Word, and the Holy Spirit is one and the same everywhere, and one is the only virgin mother, whom I love to call the church. This mother did not have milk when she was alone because when she was alone she was not a wife. But she is at the same time virgin and mother, pure as a virgin, loving as a mother. Calling her children, she nourishes them with holy milk, the Word suitable for childhood. 2. Accordingly she did not have milk, because the milk was the Word, this good and fair child, the body of Christ, which nourishes the new people which the Lord himself bore with physical pain, which the Lord himself wrapped in his precious blood. 3. O holy birth! O holy swaddling clothes! The Word is everything to the infant, father and mother and instructor and nurse. "Eat my flesh," he says, "and drink my blood" (cf. John 6:53). The Lord supplies these suitable foods for us and hands us his flesh and pours out his blood, and nothing is lacking for the children's growth. 43.1. O paradoxical mystery! We are commanded to lay aside the old and physical corruption, just like stale food, and, taking a new garment, that of Christ, to take him up if possible to receive him within ourselves and place the Savior in our hearts, so that we may annul the lusts of our flesh.

XV.

The Church "Gnostically" Conceived

CLEMENT OF ALEXANDRIA
MISCELLANIES 6.13.2

Those even now who have practiced the Lord's commandments and lived perfectly and spiritually (*gnostikos*) according to
the gospel may be enrolled in the chosen body of apostles. One is
in reality a presbyter of the church and a true deacon of the will of
God if that person does and teaches the things of the Lord, not
being appointed by human beings nor counted righteous because
a presbyter but being enrolled in the presbytery because righteous. And although that person is not honored with a throne on
earth, nevertheless he will sit among the twenty–four thrones
judging the people, as John says in the Revelation. For in reality
there is one saving covenant extending to us from the foundation
of the world but being received as a gift according to different
generations and different times. For it follows that there is one
unchangeable gift of salvation from the One God through the
One Lord which benefits "in various ways." For this reason the
"middle wall" (cf. Eph. 2:14) which separated the Greek from the
Jew has been taken away [so as to make way] for a peculiar people.
And so both have arrived "at the unity of faith" (cf. Eph. 4:13),
and there is one election from both. Now the "more elect"
among the "elect," the Scriptures say, are those who have arrived
at the perfect knowledge of the church herself and been honored
with the greatest glory both as judges and as administrators, the
twenty-four elders, equally from both Jews and Greeks, since
grace is doubled. For the ranks in the church here—bishops, presbyters, deacons—are, I think, imitations of the angelic glory and
of that plan which the Scriptures say awaits those who live in the
footsteps of the apostle in perfect righteousness according to the
gospel.

XVI.

A Third Race?

TERTULLIAN
TO THE NATIONS 1.8.1, 9—13

1.8.1. Clearly we are called a "third race. . . ." 9. Suppose the Phrygians were the first. That doesn't prove, however, that Christians are the third. For how many other series of people came after the Phrygians? But watch out lest those you call the "third race" acquire the chief place since there is no people who are not Christian. 10. And so whatever people was first, it would be no less Christian. It is laughable folly to say we are the latest and then call us the "third." 11. But we are supposed to be a "third race" as regards religion and not as regards a nation so that there are Romans, Jews, and then Christians. But what about the Greeks? 12. If they are thought to be among the religions of the Romans since Rome indeed borrowed even the gods of Greece, what about Egyptians at least? They, too, I known, have a distinct religion peculiar to themselves. 13. Besides, if those who have the third place are so monstrous, what must be thought of those who preceded them in the first and second places?

XVII.

A Distinctive People

TERTULLIAN APOLOGY 39

39.1. I will proceed then to explain the features of this Christian sect not so much to refute the evil as to show the good, and perhaps also to disclose the truth.

We are a body united by a common religious commitment and unity of teaching and hope. 2. We meet together and form a congregation so that we may wrestle with God in prayers as if in hand-to-hand combat. This violence pleases God. We pray also for the emperors, for their ministers and those in authority, for the situation of the world, for peace, for delay of the end. 3. We meet to recall the divine Scriptures if anything in the present time necessitates some sort of forewarning or acknowledgment. With the holy words certainly we feed our faith, stimulate our hope, firm up our trust, and deepen our instruction no less by the inculcations of divine precepts. 4. In this gathering also we deliver exhortations, rebukes, and divine censures. For we carry out our judgment with great seriousness as among persons who are being watched by God, and it is viewed as the highest prejudgment of the judgment to come if anyone should err so badly that that person would be removed from communion in prayer and assembly and every other holy transaction.

5. Older men who have proven themselves preside over us, having attained this honor not by money but by witness to their character, for God's business has nothing to do with money. And even though there is a kind of collection box, money is not collected from some kind of high fees as if this was a commercial religion. One day a month, or whenever one wishes and if one wishes and can, each person puts in a small donation. For

nobody is forced to give but does so voluntarily. 6. These donations are, as it were, "deposits of piety." The money is not spent, you can be sure, on sumptuous foods or drinking bouts or fancy restaurants, but to bury poor people and to meet the needs of boys and girls and destitute parents, and also old people now forced into idleness at home, and likewise those who have suffered shipwreck, and if any in the mines and on the islands and in prisons become wards of their confession insofar as it is for the sake of the church.

7. But the work of this kind of love especially brands us in the eyes of some. "Look," they say, "how they love one another," for they hate one another, "and how they are prepared to die for each other," for they are more prepared to kill each other. 8. But they also get angry at us because we think of one another as brothers and sisters, for no other reason, I think, than because among them every affectionate family name is feigned. But we are also your brothers and sisters by virtue of having one mother nature, although you are hardly human because evil brothers and sisters. 9. How much more worthy are those to be called and regarded as brothers and sisters who have known one Father, God, who have imbibed of the one Spirit of holiness, who have struggled from the one womb of the same ignorance to the one light of truth? 10. But perhaps we are thought to be less legitimate because no tragedy cries out from our fraternity or because we remain brothers and sisters despite those family possessions which destroy fraternity among you. 11. And so we who are related in mind and soul do not hesitate to share our things. We share everything except wives. 12. We give up our commonality in the only place where other persons practice commonality. They not only take possession of the wives of their friends, but they very tolerantly lend theirs to their friends, following, I think, the example of the greater and wiser of them, the Greek Socrates and the Roman Cato, who shared with friends their wives, whom they married to bear children not only for themselves but for others. 13. I don't know whether that was against their will or not, for why should they worry about chastity when their husbands gave it away so readily? What a model of Attic wisdom! What a model of Roman seriousness! The philosopher and the magistrate are pimps!

14. Is it any wonder, then, that such love as Christians have is ridiculed? For you pummel even our little suppers not only as wasteful but as infamously wicked. "The Megarians feast like they were about to die tomorrow; but they build like they were never going to die!" 15. But one sees the speck in another person's eye more easily than the log in one's own. The air is polluted with the belches of so many tribes and curias and decurias. The Salii will have to borrow money to hold their banquets. Accountants will have to tell you the costs of the Herculanean tithes and sumptuous banquets. The best of chefs is selected for the Apaturian, Dionysian, and Attic mysteries. Firemen will be called out to put out the flames of the Serapian banquet. Yet a hullaballoo is raised only about the supper room of Christians!

16. The reason for our feast is shown by its name. It is called *agape* in Greek, that is, love. However much it costs to hold it, it is worth it, an expense paid in the name of piety, since we help some of the needy with this refreshment. It is not, as among you, a case where parasites aspire to the glory of servile freedom and under control of the belly stuff themselves beyond abuse, but where greater thought is given before God to the lowly. 17. If the reason for our banquet is commendable, consider the other regulations for it in light of that reason. Because it is a religious affair, nothing vile or immodest is allowed. No one sits down before prayer to God is tasted. Each person eats only whatever is needed to satisfy hunger and drinks only whatever is appropriate for a temperate person. 18. They satisfy themselves as those who should be mindful that they must also worship God all night long; they talk about it as those who know God listens. After washing hands and bringing in lights, each person is encouraged insofar as possible to sing a hymn to God in the midst of the congregation either from the divine Scriptures or from that person's own devising. This proves how much each will drink. Prayer likewise brings the banquet to an end. 19. We depart from it not as crowds of killers or bands of vagabonds nor to get involved in lascivious acts, but rather to exercise the same care for modesty and chastity as those who gathered not so much for supper as for instruction.

20. This gathering of Christians must be condemned very deservedly as illicit, if it is like those which are illicit. It must be

condemned very deservedly if it is not unlike those which are condemned, if anyone lays against it a valid complaint such as is laid against secret factions. 21. When did we ever gather for some pernicious purpose? Assembled we are what we are when dispersed, together what we are as individuals, injuring nobody, troubling nobody. When the righteous, when the good assemble; when the pious, when the pure gather, it must not be called a faction but a curia.

XVIII.

The Church of Apostolic Tradition

TERTULLIAN *PRESCRIPTION FOR HERETICS* 20, 32, 36, 41

20.1. Christ Jesus, our Lord (if I may speak in this way for a little while), whoever he is, Son of whatever God, man and God of whatever substance, teacher of whatever faith, promisor of whatever mercy, 2. while he lived on earth, declared what he was, what he had been, what the Father's will was which he was serving, what was decreed that human beings must do. He declared this either openly to the people or privately to his disciples, from whom he chose twelve as the chief ones at his side and designated them as teachers of the nations (Mark 4:34). 3. And so when one of them was excised as he was departing to the Father after the resurrection, he ordered the other eleven to go and teach the nations, baptizing (*tinguendas*) into the Father and the Son and the Holy Spirit (Matt 28:19).

4. Immediately, therefore, the apostles—whose name means "sent"—after Matthias was chosen by lot as the twelfth in the place of Judas by authority of the prophecy which is in the Psalm of David (Acts 1:20; Ps. 109:8), received the promised power of the Holy Spirit regarding miracles and eloquence. After first witnessing throughout Judea to faith in Jesus Christ and establishing churches, from there they went forth into the world and preached the same teaching of the same faith to the nations. 5. In the same manner they founded churches in each city, from which other churches thenceforward have obtained and are obtaining day by day the tradition of faith and the seed of doctrine that they may become churches. 6. And it is as the offspring of apostolic churches that they will themselves be considered apostol-

ic. 7. Every type must be classified according to its origin. Therefore, all the churches, however many and great they may be, comprise that one first church founded by the apostles from which all of them descend. 8. Thus all of them are original and apostolic since all are one. Their peaceful communion and use of the name "brotherhood" and bond of hospitality prove they are one. 9. These are right, based on nothing but the one tradition of the same creed (*sacramentum*).

32.1. But if any heresies dare to plant themselves in the apostolic age so that they may appear to have been handed down by the apostles because they were under apostles, we can say: Let them therefore bring forth the [records] of the origins of their churches. Let them unfold the roll of their bishops, running in continuity from the beginning so that that first bishop might have some founder and forerunner among the apostles or apostolic men who, nevertheless, remained faithful to the apostles. 2. For this is how the apostolic churches transmit their lists. The church of Smyrna, for instance, records that Polycarp was called by John, and the church of Rome records that Clement was ordained by Peter. 3. In the same manner the other churches put forward those appointed to the episcopate by the apostles who transmitted the apostolic seed to them. 4. Let the heretics pretend they have anything like that. For what is unlawful for them after blasphemy? For when compared with that of the apostles, their teaching will declare by its diversity and contradictoriness that it was authored neither by an apostle nor by an apostolic person. For just as the apostles would not have taught different things among themselves, so also apostolic persons would not have taught things contrary to the apostles unless those who received their instruction from the apostles preached something else. 6. They will be challenged to adhere to this test, therefore, by those churches which, although they may not claim any founder among the apostles or apostolic persons (since they are much later and are still being founded daily), yet, since they agree in the same faith, are considered no less apostolic on account of kinship of teaching. 7. So let all the heresies, challenged by our churches to adhere to both tests [sc. succession of bishops and identity of doctrine with apostolic], prove by what means they think they are apostolic. 8. But of course they are not, and cannot prove they are what they are not. They are not accepted in peace and communion by churches which are in any way apostolic, of course, because they are in no way apostolic on account of the diversity of their creed (*sacramentum*).

36.1. Come now, you who want to exercise a healthier curiosity in the matter of your salvation. Run through the apostolic churches in which the very chairs of the apostles still preside over their places and in which their authentic letters are recited, sounding the voice and representing the face of each one. 2. If Achaia is nearest to you, you have Corinth. If you are not far from Macedonia, you have Philippi. If you can travel to Asia, you have Ephesus. But if you are close to Italy, you have Rome, from which authority has come to us also. 3. How fortunate is this church, for which the apostles poured out all their teaching with their blood! Where Peter attained to a death like the Lord's, where Paul was crowned with John's death, from where the apostle John, after he suffered no harm from immersion in boiling oil, was sent into exile on an island! 4. Let us see what she learned, what she taught, since she has established friendship with the African churches also. 5. She knows one Lord God, Creator of the universe; and Christ Jesus, Son of God the Creator of the universe; and Christ Jesus, Son of God the Creator born of the Virgin Mary, and the resurrection of the flesh. She unites the law and the prophets with the gospels and letters of the apostles, from which she drinks in her faith. She seals faith with water, clothes with the Holy Spirit, feeds with the Eucharist, urges martyrdom. And so she receives no one against this teaching. 6. This is the teaching, I no longer need tell, which was predicting future heresies but from which heresies would go forth. But they are not from it because they came into existence against it. 7. Even the rough wild olive arises necessarily from the core of the tame and rich olive; even the empty and useless fig comes out of the seed of the best and sweetest fig. 8. In the same way heresies too come from our tree, although not of our type, having a grain of truth but actually forests of lies.

41.1 I must not leave out a description of the behavior of the heretics also—how futile, how worldly, how purely human it is; without seriousness, without authority, without discipline as suits their faith. 2. In the first place it is uncertain who is a catechumen and who is a believer. They assemble at the service together; they listen together; they pray together. Even if Gentiles gather with them, they will "cast what is holy to the dogs" and "pearls [although not real pearls] before swine" (Matt. 7:6). 3. They strive for simplicity by abandonment of discipline, care for which on our part they call "pandering." They also are in communion with everybody everywhere. 4. For it doesn't matter to them how diverse their views are, so long as they agree to battle against the one truth. All are inflated. All offer knowledge. Catechumens are "perfect" before they have been instructed. 5. How shameless are the women among these heretics! They dare to teach, to argue, to exorcize, to promise cures, and perhaps even to baptize. 6. Their ordinations are thoughtless, superficial, and changeable. At one time they install the newly baptized, at another time persons caught up in worldly enterprises, at another time our apostates in order to capture them by flattery because they cannot do so by truth. 7. Nowhere is it easier to advance than in the camp of the rebels where it is meritorious merely to be there. 8. Accordingly, today one person is bishop, tomorrow someone else. Today one is a deacon who is tomorrow a reader. Today one is a presbyter who is tomorrow a layperson. For they impose priestly functions even on laypersons.

XIX.

The Montanist Church

TERTULLIAN ON PURITY 21.7–17

21.7. "But the church has the power to forgive sins," you say. I both acknowledge and do more to set this in order than you. I can invoke the Paraclete speaking in the "new prophets," saying, "The church can forgive sin, but I will not do it lest they commit other sins." 8. But what if a false prophetic spirit declared this? That is unlikely. For it would have been more than the Destroyer both to commend himself for clemency and to be indulgent to others for sin. Or even if he tried to imitate the Spirit of truth, then the Spirit of truth can certainly forgive the sin of adulterers but would not do so since it might lead many to evil.

9. I now ask your view as to where the church usurped this right. If it is because the Lord said to Peter, "Upon this rock I will build my church, and I will give you the keys of the kingdom of heaven," or "Whatever you bind or loose on earth will be bound or loosed in heaven" (Matt 16:18–19), do you therefore presume that the power of loosing and binding has devolved upon you, that is, upon every church akin to Peter? 10. What kind of person are you to subvert and change the obvious intention of the Lord, who confers this personally on Peter. "Upon *you* I will build my church," he says, and "I will give *you* the keys," not the church, and "whatever *you* loose or bind," not what *they* loose or bind.

11. For that is what the outcome also teaches. The church has been built on Peter himself, that is, through him. You see how he himself touched the key: "Men of Israel, lend your ears to what I am saying: Jesus the Nazarene, a man sent to you by God," and the rest (Acts 2:22). 12. He, then, first opened the entrance to the heavenly kingdom in Christ's baptism, wherein sins which were

60

previously "bound" are "loosed" and those which have not been "loosed" are "bound" in accord with the true salvation. Besides this, he "bound" Ananias with the bond of death and he "loosed" the lame man from his crippling defect. 13. But also in the debate as to whether or not the law should be observed, Peter was the first of all to be inspired by the Spirit and to speak out about the calling of the nations. "Now," he says, "why do you test the Lord by imposing a yoke on the brothers and sisters that neither we nor our fathers were able to bear? For we believe that we are about to obtain salvation by the grace of Jesus just as they did" (Acts 15:10–11). 14. This statement both "loosed" what had been left out by the law and "bound" what had been kept by it. The power of "loosing" and "binding" which was given to Peter, therefore, had nothing to do with forgiving the capital sins of the faithful. 15. If the Lord had commanded him to forgive a brother who sinned against him seventy times seven, he would surely have commanded him to "bind," that is, to retain, nothing afterward unless perhaps things one may have committed against the Lord, not against a brother. For the fact that sins committed against humankind are forgiven precludes the forgiveness of sins against God.

16. What, then, has this to do with the church and especially your church, O psychic? For as it was Peter's personally, so this power pertains to spiritual persons, either to an apostle or to a prophet. For the church itself is properly and principally the Spirit himself, in whom is the Trinity of the one Divinity, Father and Son and Holy Spirit. He gathers that church which the Lord said consisted of at least three persons. 17. From this time on, therefore, the whole lot of those who have agreed in this faith is thought of as the church by her Founder and Consecrator. And the church certainly will forgive sins, but the church of the Spirit through a spiritual person and not the church as a lot of bishops. For it is the right and choice of the Lord and not the servant, of God himself and not of the priest.

TERTULLIAN *AGAINST MARCION* 5.15.5–6

5.15.5. It is incumbent, therefore, on Marcion to show today in his church where there is the Spirit of his God which must not be quenched and the prophecies which must not be despised (cf.

1 Thess. 4:15–17). Even if he shows what he thinks it is, let him know that we are about to challenge whatever it is by the test of spiritual and prophetic grace and power, namely, to foretell the future and to reveal the secrets of the heart and to explain mysteries. 6. Since he could not bring forth or prove anything of the sort, we will bring forth both the Spirit and prophecies of the Creator which offer predictions according to Him. In this way we will establish what the apostle spoke about, of course, what was about to happen in the church of his God, where, as long as He exists, his Spirit also works and his promise is celebrated.

XX.

The Church as Superior to All Things Pagan

ORIGEN *AGAINST CELSUS* 3.29–30, 51; 8.74–75

3.29. . . . But the God who sent Jesus destroyed the whole conspiracy of demons and made the gospel of Jesus to take hold everywhere in the world for the conversion and rectification of humankind and caused churches to be set up everywhere in opposition to the assemblies of the superstitious and undisciplined and unrighteous. For such is the character of most of the citizens in the assemblies of the cities. But the churches of God which have been taught by Christ are "like lights in the world" when compared to the assemblies of the people among whom they live. For who would not agree that even the worst persons from the church and those least worthy in comparison with the better members are far better than people in the popular assemblies.

3.30. For the church of God, for instance, at Athens, is a meek and stable one which wants to please God, who is over everything, but the Athenian assembly is rebellious and not at all comparable to the church of God there. And you could say the same thing about the church of God which is in Corinth and the popular assembly in Corinth and, to give another example, about the church of God which is in Alexandria and the popular assembly in Alexandria. Now if the person who hears this is open-minded and investigates matters with a love for truth, that person will marvel at the one who both planned and was able to bring into existence and to sustain the churches of God everywhere, sojourning in the assemblies of the people in each city. So too would you find a council of the church of God when compared with the council in each city. Some councilors of the church are worthy to hold public office in a city of God, if there is any in the whole world. But not all public councilors everywhere have the moral character worthy of the legal superiority which they seem to exercise over the citizens. So too must we compare the ruler of the church in each city with the public ruler in the city, so that you may grasp that even among the councilors and rulers of the church of God who fail miserably and who live indifferent lives by comparison with those who are more energetic, we find, generally speaking, a more rapid progress toward the virtues than is characteristic of councilors and rulers in the cities.

3.51. If [the Cynics] are not faulted for doing this, let us see if Christians do not encourage multitudes to goodness even more and better than they. For philosophers who discourse in public do not pick and choose among their hearers, but whoever wants stands and listens. But Christians, so far as possible, first examine carefully the lives of those wanting to enroll as hearers and test them privately beforehand. Whenever the hearers, before entering the community, seem to have developed sufficient desire to live the good life, Christians introduce them at that time. Privately they form one class of those who are beginning and entering and have not yet received the sign that they have been purified. They form another class of those who have manifested their desire, insofar as possible, to strive for nothing other than what is fitting for Christians. Some of the latter have been appointed to inquire into the lives and conduct of those who join them so that they may prevent those who do anything infamous from coming to their common gathering. But those who are not of this sort they receive wholeheartedly and daily prepare them better. They use a similar procedure for those who sin, especially for those who lead gross lives, whom they exclude from the community, although, according to Celsus, they are like "those in the marketplace who put on shameful performances." Now the famous school of the Pythagoreans used to erect a tomb to those who had apostatized from their philosophy, regarding them as dead. But Christians mourn as dead those who have been overcome by ungodliness or some other sin as lost and dead to God. Yet if these persons manifest a real conversion, they welcome them back as persons raised from the dead, though after a much longer time than it took for them to enter. But they do not enroll those who have lapsed after having accepted the Word in any position of leadership and office in what is called the church of God.

8.74. If Celsus wants us to serve in the army of our country, let him know that we do this not to be seen by human beings and to obtain fame for it. For our prayers are made "in secret" in the mind itself, being sent up as by priests on behalf of our country. Christians do more good for their countries than other persons. They train citizens. They teach reverence toward the supreme God. They elevate those who have lived well in the smallest cities to some divine and heavenly city. To these it might be said, "You have been faithful in (cf. Luke 16:10; 19:17) the least city. Come also into the great one, where God stands in the assembly of gods, and judges in the midst of the gods (Ps. 82:1) and numbers you among them if you no longer die like a human being nor fall like one of the princes (cf. Ps. 82:7)."

8.75. Celsus urges us also to "hold public office in your country," if necessary, and to "do this for the sake of preservation of the law and religion." But we recognize in each city another support for the country created by God's Word and urge persons capable in speech and living a commendable life to "hold office" in the churches. We do not accept those who crave office but compel those who, because of great modesty, do not want hastily to take upon themselves the public office of the church. Those who rule well over us are under the compelling force of the great King whom we are persuaded is the Son of God, the divine Word. If those chosen or compelled to rule well in the assembly of God's country (I mean the church), and rule according to what God commands, they will do no harm to the established laws by this.

Christians do not avoid such things in order to flee the more mundane duties of life. Rather, they save themselves for a more divine and essential ministry in the church of God for the salvation of human beings. It is both necessary and right that they lead and have a concern for all, both those inside the church that they may live better day by day, and those appearing to be outside that they may embrace the sacred words and acts of worship; and thus, while they truly worship God and train as many as possible, that they may be gripped by the Word of God and the divine law and thus be united with the God who is over all through the Son of God, the Word and Wisdom and Truth and Righteousness, who united to God everyone who has been persuaded to live according to God's will in everything.

XXI.

The Double Church

31.5. One place of prayer has some charm and benefit, the spot where believers gather together in one place and, as is likely, the angels stand over the throng of believers and the power of our Lord and of holy spirits, as I think, of the dead, and surely also those who are alive, although it is not easy to say how. Now about angels we must reason as follows: if "the angel of the Lord camps round about those who fear him and will deliver them" (Ps. 34:7), and Jacob tells the truth not only about himself but also about all those who offer themselves to God, saying to the one who understands, "the angel who delivers me from all evils," it is likely that when many persons gather sincerely for the praise of Christ, each person's angel camps "around" each of "those who fear" with this person, whom he has been commissioned to protect and guide. Thus there is a double church when the saints gather, the one of human beings, the other of angels. If Raphael speaks of Tobit alone when he says that he had offered up his prayer for "a memorial" and, after him, the prayer of Sarah, who later became his daughter-in-law because of her marriage to Tobias, what must be said when many persons gather and become one body in Christ "in the same mind and with the same understanding" (1 Cor. 1:10)? Concerning the power of the Lord which is present in the church, Paul says: "When you are gathered together and my spirit with the power of the Lord Jesus" (1 Cor. 5:4), speaking about the power "of the Lord Jesus" which is associated not only with the Ephesians but also with the Corinthians. Now if Paul, still clothed with his body, thought he could make contact with his own spirit in Corinth, we must not deny that the

67

blessed ones who have departed come in the spirit more quickly than one who is present in the body in the churches. Consequently, we must not despise prayers among them, since they will have special value for those who gather sincerely with them.

6. Just as the power of Jesus and the spirit of Paul and of those like him and the angels of the Lord "camping around each of the saints" meet and gather with those who join together sincerely, so must we suppose that if anyone is unworthy of the holy angel and gives himself up to that angel, the devil, so as to sin and wickedly disregard God, such a person, there being few like him, will never escape the notice of the angels who watch over the church in service of the divine will and bring to the attention of the majority the faults of such a person. This is made clear in Isaiah as the Lord says, "not even if you come to let me see you," for, he says, "I will turn away my eyes from you; even if you pray much, I will not listen to you" (Isa. 1:15). For perhaps instead of the double gathering of saintly human beings and blessed angels, there is again a double gathering at the same place of godless human beings and wicked angels. And over a gathering of such it might be said by both the holy angels and holy human beings, "I did not sit with the council of vanity, and I did not enter with the transgressors. I hated the assembly of evil-doers, and I will not sit with the ungodly" (Ps. 26:4–5).

XXII.

The Church in the Bishops

CYPRIAN ON THE UNITY
OF THE CHURCH

1. Since the Lord warns and says, "You are the salt of the earth" (Matt. 5:13) and since he orders us to be simple and innocent and yet prudent in our simplicity, what is more fitting, dear friends, than to keep our eyes open and watching with anxious heart to understand the deceptions of the crafty enemy and beware lest we who have put on Christ, the Wisdom of God the Father, seem less than wise in guarding our salvation. For we must not fear only persecution and things which proceed by open assault to ruin and destroy the servants of God. Caution is easier where fear is evident, and the mind prepares itself for conflict when the adversary declares himself. An enemy must be feared and guarded against more when he creeps in secretly, when he crawls in by secret openings while deceiving one under the image of peace. From this he gets the name of serpent. That is always his cunning. That is the blind and secret deception for ensnaring a person. Thus from the beginning of the world on has he deceived. Flattering with lying words he has deceived the uninstructed soul by careless credulity. Thus when he attempted to tempt the Lord himself, he came upon him secretly, as if he might creep up on him a second time and deceive him. Nevertheless, he was spotted and beaten back and indeed knocked down because he was recognized and unmasked.

2. From this we were given an example that we should flee the way of the old humanity and walk in the footsteps of the conquering Christ lest carelessly we return again into the trap of death rather than attain to the immortality won for us by foresee-

ing the danger. Yet how can we attain immortality unless we keep the commandments of Christ by which death is fought and overcome? Christ himself warns and says, "If you want to enter into life, keep the commandments" (Matt. 19:17). And again, "If you do what I command you, I no longer will call you servants but friends" (John 15:14, 15). Indeed, he calls strong and firm those who are founded securely upon a rock, who stand fixed with immovable and unshaken firmness against all the tempests and winds of the age. "Who hears my words and does them," he says, "I will compare to a wise man who builds his house upon a rock. The rain fell, the floods came, the winds blew and beat against that house, and it did not fall. For it was founded upon a rock" (Matt. 7:24, 25).

We ought therefore to stand upon, learn, and do his words, whatever he both taught and did. How else can anyone say that she believes in Christ who does not do what Christ commanded us to do? Or how will she attain the reward of faith who does not want to keep faith with the commandments? Such a person must of necessity totter and go astray, and, seized by the spirit of error, be whirled like dust which the wind blows up. One who does not hold the truth of the way of salvation will not advance in his walk to salvation.

3. We must beware, dear friends, not only of what is open and evident but also of cunning trickery and subtle deceit. What is more cunning or more subtle than that the enemy who was unmasked and knocked down at the advent of Christ—after light came to the Gentiles and the sun poured out its light for the salvation of humankind, so that the deaf received news of the grace of the Spirit, the blind opened their eyes to God, the weak grew strong with eternal health, the lame ran to the church, the deaf prayed with clear voices and prayers—seeing idols abandoned and his seats and temples deserted by a wonderful number of believers, should think up a new deception that he might deceive the careless under the very title of the name "Christian"? He invented heresies and schisms by which he might subvert the faith, corrupt the truth, and rend the unity of the church. Those he cannot hold to the blindness of the old way, he surrounds and deceives by leading them astray on a new road. He snatches people from the church itself and, just as they seem to have drawn

near to the light and to have escaped the world's night, he pulls
the shades down again. So those standing neither with the gospel
of Christ nor its observance and law call themselves Christians.
Walking in darkness, they think they have the light. The Adversary flatters and deceives. He is the one who, according to the
word of the Apostle, changes himself into an angel of light and
adorns his servants like servants of righteousness. The latter
declare that night is day, death salvation, despair a garb for hope,
infidelity a pretext for faith, antichrist the same as Christ, so that
they render truth useless by the subtle use of plausible lies. This is
what happens, dear friends, when we do not return to the source
of truth nor seek the head nor keep the teaching of the heavenly
teacher.

4. If anyone ponders and weighs these things, there is no need
for a long discussion and argument. It is easy to prove the faith by
a summary of the truth. The Lord says to Peter: "I tell you that you
are Peter, and upon this rock I will build my church, and the gates
of hell will not overcome it. I will give you the keys of the kingdom of heaven and whatever you bind on earth will be bound
also in heaven, and whatever you loose on earth will be loosed
also in heaven" (Matt. 16:18–19). And again he says to him after
the resurrection: "Feed my sheep" (John 21:15). (A later edition
added: "He builds his church upon that one, and commands him
to feed his sheep.") Now he shares his power equally with all the
apostles after his resurrection, saying: "Just as the Father has sent
me, I also send you. Receive my Holy Spirit. If you forgive the sins
of anyone, they will be forgiven; if you retain the sins of anyone,
they will be retained" (John 20:20–23). Nevertheless, in order to
make unity evident, by his own authority he arranged for the
source of this same unity to begin with one person. Certainly the
other apostles were also what Peter was, endued with an equal
share both of honor and power. But the beginning takes its point
of departure from unity so that the church of Christ may be manifested as one. (The later edition adds: "And primacy is given Peter,
so that one church of Christ and one chair of the bishop may be
shown. All are pastors, but one flock is shown which is fed by all
the apostles with unanimous agreement.") In the Song of Songs
also the Holy Spirit signifies that the Church is one from the person of the Lord, saying: "One is my dove, my perfect one. She is

her mother's only one, the choice one of the one who begot her" (Song of Sol. 6:9). Does a person who does not keep this unity of the church believe that he keeps the faith? Does a person who battles and resists the church (the later edition adds: "who deserts the chair of Peter upon which the church was founded") have confidence that he is in the church when the blessed apostle Paul teaches the same thing and shows the mystery of the unity, saying: "There is one body and one spirit, one hope of your calling, one Lord, one faith, one baptism, one God" (Eph. 4:4–6)?

5. This unity we ought firmly to keep and to champion, especially we bishops, who preside in the church so that we may prove that the episcopate itself is also one and undivided. Let no one deceive the brotherhood with a lie. Let no one corrupt the truth of faith with a faithless sham. There is one episcopate, a part of which is held for the whole by each bishop. The church is also one, although it spreads farther and farther into a mass of churches with ever growing fruitfulness, as the sun has many rays but one light, and many branches on a tree but one hardwood tree held firm by the clinging root. When many streams flow from one spring, although the number seems to be increased by the amount of water pouring out, still unity is preserved at the source. Pluck a ray of sun from the body; its unity allows no division of the light. Break a branch from a tree; broken, it will not be able to bud. Cut off a stream from the spring; cut off, it dries up. So also the church. Flooded by the light of the Lord, it spreads its rays throughout the world. Yet the light which is poured out everywhere is one, and the unity of the body is not broken. With her rich supply she extends her branches throughout the earth, wider and wider she expands her rippling streams. Yet there is one head and one source and one mother who is endlessly fertile. We are born from her womb, nourished by her milk, and animated by her spirit.

6. The bride of Christ cannot become an adulteress. She is undefiled and chaste. She knows one home. She guards the sanctity of one bedroom with purity and chastity. It is she who keeps us for God. It is she who seals for the kingdom the children whom she has begotten. Anyone who has separated from the church and joined himself to an adulteress is cut off from the things promised to the church. Anyone who leaves the church of

Christ will not obtain the rewards of Christ. He is a stranger, an outcast, an enemy. Whoever does not have the church as a mother no longer has God as a father. If anyone who was outside Noah's ark could escape, then one who was outside the church will escape. The Lord warns and says, "whoever is not with me is against me, and one who does not gather with me scatters" (Matt. 12:30). One who breaks the peace and harmony of Christ acts against Christ. One who gathers elsewhere outside the church scatters. The Lord says, "I and the Father are one" (John 10:30). And again it is written concerning the Father and the Son and the Holy Spirit, "And these three are one" (1 John 5:7). Does anyone believe that this unity which comes from divine strength and is united in celestial mysteries can be split in the church and cut off by the divorce of clashing wills? One who does not keep this unity does not keep God's law, nor faith in the Father and Son, nor life and salvation.

7. This mystery of unity, this bond of harmony which holds together inseparably, is proven when in the Gospel the cloak of our Lord Jesus Christ is not divided or split at all. Rather, the whole garment is taken and the unspoiled and undivided robe is possessed by those casting lots for the garment of Christ to determine who should wear it. The divine Scripture says, "But because his robe was not sewn from above but was woven throughout, they said to one another: 'Let us not split it, but let us cast lots for it to determine who gets it' " (John 10:23–24). It bore the unity which comes "from above," that is, which comes from heaven and from the Father, which could not be split at all by taking and possessing it but kept its complete and firm strength without division. Anyone who splits and divides the church of Christ cannot possess Christ's clothing. On the contrary, when, as Solomon was dying, his kingdom and people were split, Ahijah the prophet met king Jeroboam in the field and tore his clothing into twelve pieces, saying, "You take ten pieces because the Lord says: 'Behold, I am splitting the kingdom from the hand of Solomon and I will give you ten scepters. And he will have two scepters for the sake of my servant David and for the sake of the city of Jerusalem, which I have chosen to put my name there" (1 Kings 11:31ff.). When the twelve tribes of Israel were being split, the prophet Ahijah divided his clothing. But because

the people of Christ cannot be divided, his robe, which was woven in one piece throughout, was not divided by those who possessed it. Undivided, joined together, connected, it proves the inseparable unity of our people, we who have put on Christ. By the mystery and sign of his garment he has declared the unity of the church.

8. Who, then, is so wicked and treasonous, so crazy with the fury of discord, as either to believe the unity of the church, the garment of the Lord, the church of Christ, can be split or to dare to split it? Christ warns in his gospel and teaches, saying, "And there will be one flock and one shepherd" (John 10:16). Does anyone think there can be in one place either many shepherds or many flocks? Likewise, the apostle Paul, urging this same unity upon us, begs and urges, saying, "I beg you, brothers and sisters, by the name of our Lord Jesus Christ, that all of you say the same thing and that there be no schisms among you, but that you may be joined together in the same mind and in the same thoughts" (1 Cor. 1:10). And he says also, "Hold one another up in love, striving to keep the unity of the Spirit in the bond of peace" (Eph. 4:2–3). Do you think one can stand and live when one withdraws from the church and establishes other chairs and different houses for himself, since it was said to Rahab, in whom the church was prefigured: "Gather your father and your mother and your brothers and the entire household of your father into your own home with yourself, and everyone who goes outside the door of your house will be liable for himself" (Josh. 2:18–19)? Similarly, the sacrament of the Passover in the book of Exodus contains nothing else than that the lamb, which is killed as a type of Christ, be eaten in one house. God says, "It will be eaten in one house; you will not throw the flesh outside the house" (Exod. 12:46). The flesh of Christ and the holy thing of the Lord cannot be thrown outside, and there is no home for believers except the one church. The Holy Spirit marks clearly this house, this inn of unanimity, in the Psalms, saying, "God, who makes us live together in unanimity in one house" (Ps. 68:6). In the house of God, in the church of Christ they live in unanimity. They continue in harmony and simplicity.

9. This is also why the Holy Spirit comes in the dove. It is a simple and joyous creature, not bitter with gall, not fierce and apt to bite, not ready to rip one with violent claws. It loves human

hospitality and knows the fellowship of one home. When they bear offspring, they bring them up together. When they fly about, they stay with one another in flight. They spend their lives in united behavior. They acknowledge the harmony of peace with a mutual kiss. They fulfill the law of unanimity in all things. This is the simplicity which must be known in the church, the love which must be practiced, so that the love of the brotherhood may imitate the doves and kindliness and gentleness be equal to those of lambs and sheep. What place has the ferocity of wolves and the madness of dogs and the deadly poison of snakes and the cruel fury of wild animals in the breast of Christians? We must rejoice when such persons are separated from the church lest they prey upon the doves or the sheep of Christ with their cruel and poisonous contact. Bitterness cannot be united and mixed with sweetness, darkness with light, storm with calm, war with peace, sterility with fertility, drought with springs of water, tempest with tranquility. Let no one think that good persons can leave the church. Wind does not blow away the grain nor does a hurricane overturn a deeply rooted tree. It is the empty husks which are blown away by the tempest, and feeble trees which are overturned by the twisting of the whirlwind. John the apostle curses and strikes these, saying, "They went out from us, but they were not of us. If they had been of us, they would certainly have remained with us" (1 John 2:19).

10. Hence heresies have frequently occurred and still occur, since a perverted mind has no peace and discordant perfidy does not keep unity. But the Lord permits and allows this to happen, inasmuch as each person's will remains free, so that while the test of truth searches our hearts and our minds, the sound faith of those who are proven may shine with a clear light. Through the apostle the Holy Spirit warns us, saying, "There must be heresies so that those who are proven may be evident among you" (1 Cor. 11:19). In this manner the faithful are proven, the faithless are unmasked, and the souls of the just and the unjust are distinguished already before the judgment day and the husks are separated from the wheat. The latter are the ones who install themselves over their rash associates without divine appointment, who appoint themselves as bishops without any law of ordination, who take the name of the bishops without anyone

giving them the episcopate. In the Psalms the Holy Spirit describes them as "sitting in the chair of pestilence" (Ps. 1:1). They are plagues and blights on the faith, deceiving with the mouth of the serpent and vomiting out deadly poisons with plague-bearing tongues as devices for corrupting the truth, whose word "crawls like a cancer" (2 Tim. 2:17) and whose writing pours a deadly virus into the breasts and hearts of individuals.

11. Against people of this type the Lord cries out. He holds his erring people back from them and recalls them, saying, "Don't listen to the words of the false prophets since the visions of their heart invalidate them. They speak, but not from the mouth of the Lord. They say to those who throw away the word of God: 'You and all those who proceed according to their own wills will have peace. No evil will happen to anyone who proceeds in the error of his heart.' I have not spoken to them; yet they themselves have prophesied. If they had stood in my council (*substantia*) and listened to my words and taught my people, I would have turned them from their evil thoughts" (Jer. 23:16–21). The Lord again calls attention to these same persons, saying, "They have forsaken me, the fountain of living water, and dug out for themselves cracked cisterns which cannot hold water" (Jer. 2:13). When there cannot be more than one baptism, they think they can baptize. Having deserted the fountain of life, they promise the gift of living and saving water. People are not cleansed there; rather, they are defiled. Sins are not purged there; rather, they are piled higher. That "birth" bears children not for God but for the devil. Born through a lie, they do not lay hold on the promises of the truth. Procreated from faithlessness, they lose the gift of faith. They who have shattered the peace of the Lord with the fury of discord cannot come to the reward of peace.

12. Let certain persons not deceive themselves with empty interpretation of the Lord's statement that "Wherever two or three are gathered in my name, I am with them" (Matt. 18:20). Corrupters and false interpreters of the gospel put down the last part and glide over the first, mindful of one part but deceitfully suppressing the other. Just as they have themselves split the church, so they split the meaning of one passage. For the Lord was urging agreement and peace among his disciples. "I tell you," he says, "that if two of you agree about anything on earth, what-

ever you ask will be granted you by my Father, who is in heaven. For wherever two or three are gathered in my name, I am with them" (Matt. 18:20). This shows that most is given not for the great number but for the agreement of those who pray. "If two of you will agree on earth," he says. He put agreement first. He put peaceful harmony first. He taught us to agree faithfully and firmly. But how can one agree with someone who does not agree with Christ's body, the church, and with the whole brotherhood? How can two or three gather in the name of Christ when they are separated from Christ and from his gospel? For we have not withdrawn from them; rather, they have withdrawn from us, since heresies and schisms have been born later when they established separate meetings for themselves and abandoned the head and source of truth. However, the Lord tells his church and those who are in the church that they can obtain what they ask from the divine majesty if they agree, if they pray with one mind when two or three gather as he commanded and advised. "Wherever two or three are gathered in my name," he says, "I am with them," that is, with the simple and peaceful, with those who fear God and keep God's commandments. He said he is with those "two or three" especially when he was with the three children in the fiery furnace. Because they remained simple toward God and of one mind among themselves, he refreshed their spirits in the midst of the flames which encircled them "with the spirit of dew." In like manner he was present with the two apostles when they were shut up in prison because they were simple and of one mind. When the prison doors were opened, he placed them again in the market place that they might deliver the Word which they preached faithfully to the crowd. When he places among his precepts the statement, "where two or three are gathered in my name, I am with them," therefore, he does not divide people from the church, he who established and created the church. Rather, reproving the faithless for discord and commending the faithful for peace with his own voice, he shows that he is more fully present with two or three praying with one mind than with many schismatics and that more can be obtained by the harmonious petition of a few than by the unharmonious prayer of many.

13. When he gave the rule of prayer, moreover, he added: "And when you stand and pray, forgive whatever you hold against

someone so that your Father who is in heaven may forgive you your sins" (Mark 11:25). And he recalls a person going to the altar to offer a sacrifice with discord in his heart and orders him first to be reconciled with his brother and then to return with peace to make an offering to God. For God did not look with favor on Cain's offering, for one who did not have peace with his brother on account of the divisiveness of jealousy, could not have God at peace with him. What sort of peace, then, do those who hate brothers and sisters promise themselves? What kind of sacrifices do those who envy the priests think they celebrate? Or do those who gather outside the church of Christ think that Christ is with them when they gather?

14. Though such persons should be slain confessing the name, this stain is not washed away even by blood. Responsibility for discord is so grave and inexpiable it cannot be washed away even by suffering. A person who is not in the church cannot be a martyr. One who forsakes her who is about to reign could never attain to the kingdom. Christ gave us peace. He taught us to be agreeable and of one mind. He commanded that the bonds of love and charity be kept uncorrupted and undefiled. One who has not kept fraternal love, therefore, cannot claim martyrdom. The apostle Paul teaches and attests this when he says, "And if I have such faith as to move mountains but do not have love, I am nothing. And if I give all my possessions to feed the poor and surrender my body to be burned, but do not have love, I am not benefited. Love is patient. Love is kind. Love does not envy. It does not behave improperly. It is not puffed up. It is not irritable. It does not think evil. It loves everything, believes everything, hopes everything, endures everything. Love never fails" (1 Cor. 13:2–5, 7–8). "Love," he says, "never fails." For it will always be in the kingdom. It will last forever in the unity of a brotherhood which holds together in itself. Discord can never attain to the kingdom of heaven, to the rewards of Christ, who said, "This is my commandment, that you love one another just as I have loved you" (John 15:12). One who has defiled the love of Christ with faithless schism could not fulfill this. A person who does not have love does not have God. Listen to the blessed apostle John. "God is love," he says. "Who abides in love abides in God, and God abides in that person" (1 John 4:16). They cannot abide with God who

are not of one mind in the church of God. Though they give themselves up to burn in flames of fire or lay down their lives as prey for wild animals, they will not have the crown of faith but the penalty of faithlessness, nor the glorious end of religious virtue but a death of despair. Such a person can be killed but not crowned. She may profess that she is a Christian as the devil often pretends to be Christ. As the Lord himself forewarns, "Many will come in my name, saying, 'I am the Christ,' and they will deceive many" (Mark 13:6). Just as that person is not Christ, even though she deceives in the name, so also one who does not persist in the truth of his gospel and of faith cannot be regarded as a Christian.

15. Although it is a high and wonderful thing certainly to prophesy and to cast out demons and to perform great miracles on earth, one who possesses all these gifts does not attain the heavenly kingdom unless that person walks on the straight and just road. The Lord declares that when he says, "For many will say to me on that day, 'Lord, Lord, have we not prophesied in your name and cast out demons in your name and performed great miracles in your name?' And then I will say to them, 'I do not know you. Depart from me, you who do evil' " (Matt. 7:22–23). Justice is needed if one is to find mercy before God as judge. His precepts and warnings must be obeyed if we are to receive mercy for our merits. When the Lord was pointing out in his gospel the way of our hope and faith with a brief summary, he says, "The Lord, your God, is one God," and "Love the Lord, your God, with all your heart and all your soul and all your strength." This is the first commandment. And the second is like it: "Love your neighbor as yourself. On these two commandments hang the law and the prophets" (Mark 12:29–31). In his teaching he taught both unity and love. He summarized all the prophets and the law in two commandments. But how does one preserve unity, how does one guard or think about love, who, crazy with the rage of discord, splits the church, destroys the faith, disturbs the peace, weakens love, profanes the sacrament?

16. The evil, faithful friends, began long ago. But now its cruel havoc has increased and the poisonous plague of heretical perversity and schisms have begun to arise and gain vigor. For that is what has to happen at the end of the world, as the Holy Spirit prophesies and forewarns us through the apostle. "In the last

days," he says, "grievous times will come. People will be self-serving, proud, puffed up, covetous, blasphemers, disobedient to parents, ungrateful, impious, without natural affection, implacable, informers, unchaste, harsh, not loving good, traitors, wanton, inflated with folly, lovers of pleasure rather than God, holding the form of religion but denying its power. Some of them are the ones who sneak into homes and prey on foolish women burdened by sins who are led by various desires, always burning and yet never able to arrive at a knowledge of the truth. Just as Jannes and Jambres opposed Moses, so also these oppose the truth. But they will not go much farther, for their foolishness will be evident to all, just as theirs was" (2 Tim. 3:1–9). Whatever was foretold is now fulfilled. As the end of the world approaches, it will come about equally for a testing of both human beings and times. As the adversary rages more and more, error deceives, folly extols, envy kindles, greed blinds, wickedness corrupts, pride puffs us, discord causes bitterness, anger plunges recklessly on.

17. Yet the excessive and sudden unfaithfulness of many should not move or disturb us, but rather it should confirm our faith in the truth of the matter which has been declared ahead of time. When some begin to be such because it was predicted, let other brothers and sisters beware of persons of that type because it has also been predicted beforehand, as the Lord instructs, "But you beware. Lo, I have told you everything beforehand" (Mark 13:23). I beg you, brothers and sisters, avoid such persons, and remove your heart and ears as far as you can from such dangerous discussion, like contact with death, as it is written: "Hedge your ears with thorns, and don't listen to an evil tongue" (cf. Eccles. 28:24–26). And again: "Evil conversation corrupts good manners" (1 Cor. 15:33). The Lord teaches and admonishes us to withdraw from such. "The blind,' he says, "are leaders of the blind. But if a blind person leads a blind person, both fall into a ditch" (Matt. 15:14). Whoever has become separated from the church must be shunned and fled from. This type of person is perverted, sins, and is self-condemned. Or does a person who acts against Christ's priests and withdraws himself from the company of his clergy and people seem to be with Christ himself? That person bears arms against the church and fights against the

ordinance of God. An enemy of the altar, a rebel against Christ's sacrifice, a traitor to the faith, a blasphemer of religion, a disobedient servant, a wicked son, a hostile brother—this person dares to despise the bishops and forsake God's priests and set up another altar, to profane the truth of the Lord's offering by false sacrifices. He does not know that anyone who struggles against the ordinance of God is punished by divine chastisement on account of his reckless audacity.

18. Thus Korah, Dathan, and Abiram paid penalties immediately for their efforts to claim for themselves the right to sacrifice as priests in opposition to Moses and Aaron. Its bonds broken, the earth opened up into a deep cave, and the hole in the gaping soil swallowed them alive where they stood. The wrath of an angry God struck not only those who were responsible for this, but the fire streaming from the Lord also consumed with quick vengeance the two hundred and fifty other participants and allies in this same uprising who were cohorts with them in this audacity. This warns and shows, of course, that whatever wicked deeds were attempted by human will in order to destroy the ordinance of God are done in opposition to God. So, too, King Uzziah was confounded by the divine wrath and defiled by a kind of leprosy on his forehead when he carried the censer and violently took upon himself the offering of a sacrifice contrary to the law of God, despite the opposition of Azariah the priest, and would not yield and withdraw. He was branded by the offended Lord on the part of the body where those who obtain the favor of the Lord are sealed. The sons of Aaron, who placed strong fire on the altar which the Lord did not command, were immediately blotted out in the sight of the avenging Lord.

19. Those who seek strange doctrines and introduce teachings devised by human beings, despising what God has handed down, are the ones whom they naturally imitate and follow. The Lord rebukes and castigates them in his gospel, saying, "You reject the commandment of God so that you may establish your own tradition" (Mark 7:9). This is a worse offense than those who fell in persecution seem to have committed, yet who do penance for that offense and entreat God, making full satisfaction. In the latter the church is sought and asked for, in the former it is combatted. In one case there may have been the use of force, in the other

the will is gripped by wickedness. In one case the one who has fallen has harmed only himself, in the other one who has tried to make a heresy or schism deceives many and drags them down with himself. In one case there is loss of one soul, in the other danger for many. Certainly the lapsed person understands that he has sinned and laments and weeps about it. The other person, puffed up in his breast and pleased with his own sins, separates children from their mother, solicits sheep from their shepherd, and upsets the mysteries of God. Although the lapsed sinned once, this person sins daily. Finally, the lapsed person who has obtained martyrdom later can receive the promises of the kingdom, but this person, should he be killed outside the church, cannot attain to the rewards which belong to the church.

20. No one should be amazed, dear brothers and sisters, that some of the confessors have reached the point that some of them also sin so wickedly and grievously. Not even confession makes one immune to the devil's tricks or safeguards one living in the world with perpetual security against worldly temptations, dangers, attacks, and assaults. Otherwise we would never again see among confessors deceptions, fornication, and adultery such as we now are grieving about among some. Whoever the confessor, that person is not greater or better or dearer to God than Solomon. As long as he walked in the paths of the Lord, he was endowed with grace he had received from the Lord. Yet after he abandoned the way of the Lord, he also lost the grace of the Lord. Moreover, it is written: "Hold on to what you have lest another take your crown" (Rev. 3:11). Certainly the Lord would not threaten that he might take away the crown of righteousness unless when justice goes, the crown must go too.

21. Confession is the beginning of glory, it does not deserve a crown at once. It does not perfect praise, but it imitates honor, for it is written: "Whoever perseveres to the end will be saved" (Matt. 10:22). Whatever has preceded the end is a step by which one climbs to the summit of salvation. It is not the end where the highest peak is reached. One is a confessor, but after confession the danger is greater, for the adversary has been provoked more. If one is a confessor, that person ought to stand still more firmly with the gospel of the Lord, inasmuch as she has obtained glory from the Lord through the gospel. For the Lord says, "Much is

required of one who is given much, and more service is demanded of one to whom greater honor is ascribed" (Luke 12:48). Let no one perish because of the example of a confessor. Let no one learn injustice, insolence, or unfaithfulness from a confessor's behavior. If one is a confessor, that person should be humble, peaceable, modest, and disciplined in conduct, so that whoever is called a confessor of Christ may imitate the Christ she confesses. For Christ says, "Whoever exalts himself will be humbled and whoever humbles himself will be exalted" (Luke 18:14). Because the Word and Power and Wisdom of God, the Father, humbled himself on earth, he has himself been exalted. How, then, can he love exaltation, who commanded us in his law to be humble and himself received from the Father a most excellent name as a prize for humility? One is a confessor of Christ only if the majesty and dignity of Christ are not blasphemed later by him. Let not the tongue that has confessed Christ speak evil or be disruptive. Let it not be heard to rumble with abuses and quarrels. Let it not spew out the poison of a serpent against brothers and priests of God after words of praise. If one should afterwards become culpable and hateful, waste his confession by evil behavior, defile his life by base filthiness, and finally, exchange his original faith for later faithlessness, forsaking the church in which he became a confessor and splitting the harmony of unity, that person cannot flatter himself on the basis of his confession by thinking he has been chosen for the prize of glory when, for this very reason, he deserves punishments all the more.

22. The Lord chose Judas to be one of the apostles, yet Judas later betrayed the Lord. Even so, the firm faith of the apostle did not fail because the traitor Judas defected from this company. Similarly, in this case also, the holiness and dignity of the confessors have not bee immediately diminished because the faith of some of them has been shattered. The blessed apostle Paul says in his letter, "What if some of them fell from the faith? Has their unfaithfulness destroyed the effectiveness of God's faithfulness? Never! For God is true, even if every human being is a liar" (Rom. 3:3–4). The larger and better part of the confessors stands fast in the strength of their faith and in the truth of the Lord's law and teaching. They do not depart from the peace of the church who are mindful that they have obtained grace in the church by virtue

of God's favor. For this reason they obtain fuller praise for their faith because, separated from the faithlessness of those who were fellow confessors, they have drawn back from contact with the offense. But illuminated by the light of the gospel and suffused with the pure and white light of the Lord, they are as worthy of praise for preserving the peace of Christ as they have been victorious in their encounter with the devil.

23. Dear brothers and sisters, my desire, my counsel, and my plea is that, if possible, not one of the brothers and sisters be lost and that the rejoicing mother may draw to her bosom one body of people who agree with one another. Yet if this saving counsel could not recall to the way of salvation some leaders of the schisms and creators of faction who persist in their blind and obstinate madness, at least you others, who have either been caught through naiveté or led into error or deceived by some very clever trick, should free yourselves from the snares of deceit, liberate your wandering steps from errors, and recognize the right way to heaven. The voice of the apostle bears witness. "We command you in the name of our Lord Jesus Christ," he says, "to withdraw from all brothers and sisters who proceed in a disorderly way and not according to the tradition which they received from us" (2 Thess. 3:6). And again he says, "Let no one deceive you by empty words, for the wrath of God is coming upon the children of disobedience for this reason. Don't get involved with them, therefore" (Eph. 5:6–7). We must withdraw or rather flee from those who stray lest, if anyone joins those who behave badly and walks down the path of error and crime, that person wander from the true path and also become liable for the same crime. There is one God, one Christ, one church of Christ, one faith, and a people fastened together in solid corporate unity by the glue of concord. This unity cannot be split nor the one body divided by tearing up the structure. It cannot be broken into fragments by tearing and mangling its viscera. Whatever has been separated from the womb cannot live and breathe outside it; it loses the essence of health.

24. The Holy Spirit warns us, saying, "Who is it who wants life and loves to see the best days? Restrain your tongue from evil, and let not your lips speak deceptively. Avoid evil and do good. Seek peace and pursue it" (Ps. 34:13–15). A child of peace ought to

seek peace and pursue it. Whoever knows and loves the bond of love ought to restrain her tongue from the evil of faction. Among his divine commandments and salutary teaching, as he approached his death, the Lord added this: "Peace I leave with you. My peace I give you" (John 14:27). He gave us this inheritance. He promised all his pledged gifts and rewards for the keeping of peace. If we are heirs of Christ, let us remain in the peace of Christ. If we are children of God, we ought to be peacemakers. "Blessed are the peacemakers," he says, "for they will be called children of God" (Matt. 5:9). Children of God ought to be peacemakers, gentle in heart, simple in speech, agreeable in affection, faithfully binding themselves together with the words of unanimity.

25. Such unanimity once existed under the apostles. In this manner the new company of believers, keeping the Lord's commandments, preserved its love. This is proven by the divine Scripture which says: "And the multitude of those who believed were acting with one soul and mind" (Acts 4:32). And again: "And they were all persisting with one mind in prayer with the women and Mary, the mother of Jesus, and his brothers" (Acts 1:14). For that reason they were praying effective prayers and could obtain with confidence whatever they asked of the Lord's mercy.

26. But among us unanimity has diminished just as liberality in good deeds has been broken. In those days they were selling their houses and farms, and laying up treasures for themselves in heaven, they were offering the proceeds to the apostles to be distributed for the use of the needy. But now we do not even give a tithe from our patrimony, and we buy and increase our possessions rather than selling them as the Lord ordered. As a result, the vigor of faith has dried up among us and the strength of believers has grown faint. Therefore the Lord, looking at our times, says in his Gospel: "Do you think the Son of man will find faith on earth when he comes?" (Luke 18:8) We see that what he predicted has happened. There is no faith in the fear of the Lord, in the law of righteousness, in love, in work. No one thinks about fear of things to come. No one meditates on the Day of the Lord, the wrath of God, the punishment about to befall the unbeliever, and the eternal torments established for unbelief. Our conscience does not fear what it would fear if it believed because it doesn't

believe at all. If it believed, it would also fear. If it feared, it would escape.

27. Let us arouse ourselves as much as we can, dear brothers and sisters, break off the slumber of our old sloth, and keep our eyes open to observe and carry out the Lord's commands. Let us be the kind of persons he commanded us to be when he says: "Let your loins be girded and your lights burning, and you be like people waiting for their lord when he returns from the wedding so that they may open to him when he comes and knocks. Blessed are those servants whom the Lord will find awake when he comes" (Luke 12:35–37). We ought to be girded up lest, when the day of the campaign comes, he find us hindered and unready. Let our light shine and gleam with good works that it may guide us out of this world's night to the light of eternal glory. Always careful and cautious, let us await the Lord's sudden advent so that, when he knocks, our faith may receive the prize of watchfulness from the Lord. If these commandments are kept and these warnings and precepts observed, we cannot be caught sleeping by the deceitful devil; we will reign with Christ as watchful servants.

XXIII.

Corpus Christianum

EUSEBIUS *THE LIFE OF
CONSTANTINE* 3.1.1–3.3.3; 3.11–12; 4.24

3.1.1. The envy which despises good, maligning the good things happening to the church, continued to stir up storms and internal strife in a time of peace and joy. But the emperor, the friend of God, was not neglecting the duties incumbent upon him. Rather, he was doing everything possible to oppose the horrors perpetrated a little while ago by the cruel tyrant, winning every battle against the enemy. 2. Having forsaken the true God, they were compelling us by every compulsion to worship those which aren't gods; but he, proving that these false gods do not exist in deeds as well as words, was urging us to make known the only true God. They were ridiculing the Christ of God with blasphemous words, but he was inscribing the very thing which the godless especially derided upon his standard as a safeguard, revering it as an emblem of Christ's passion. They were persecuting and driving the servants of God out of house and home; but he was recalling all of them and restoring them to their own homes. 3. They were heaping dishonors on them; but he was making them honorable and enviable to all. They were illegally seizing the property of the godly and selling it; but he was enriching it with greater gifts and giving it back. They were spreading abroad hurtful slanders against the leaders of the church with their decrees; but he was lifting them up and elevating them to a position of honor and making them more illustrious persons by his edicts and laws. 4. They were demolishing the houses of prayer, tearing them down to the ground; but he was decreeing that new ones should be erected and those which still existed

enlarged at the expense of the imperial treasury. They were order-
ing the inspired Scriptures to be burned and utterly destroyed;
but he was commanding that the number of these be increased
and lavishly adorned at imperial expense. 5. They were strictly
forbidding the bishops to convene synods anywhere; but he was
assembling them from all nations in his court and counting them
worthy not only to enter his palace but even to stay in his private
apartment and eat at the imperial table. They were honoring the
demons with offerings; but he was exposing their error and continually dispensing the useless materials of their sacrifices to
those able to use them. They were commanding that the temples
be richly adorned; but he was tearing down to the ground those
which were counted especially worthy by the demon worship-
pers. 6. They were subjecting God's martyrs to the most shameful punishments; but he, enlightening the persecutors with a
punishment God deserves to impose, did not cease honoring the
memory of the holy martyrs of God. They were driving worship-
pers from the royal palace; but he was putting more and more
trust in them, knowing that they were of better disposition and
more faithful than any others. 7. Victims of avarice, they were
enslaving their souls to the greed of Tantalus; but he, unlocking
all the royal treasures with imperial majesty, was distributing
them with rich and generous gesture. They were committing
thousands upon thousands of murders in order to seize and
divide the property of their victims; but in Constantine's time
every sword was taken away as useless for justice throughout the
empire, as both people and politicians were being governed by
the law of their fathers rather than by compulsion. 8. Having
seen this surely, one would say that some new and fresh era seems
now at last to have appeared, with a strange light shining with full
force on the human race, and confess that it is all God's work, for
God has brought forth this godly emperor to oppose the multitude of godless ones.

3.2.1. Since they dared to perpetrate against the church such
atrocities as were never seen nor heard of, it is understandable
that God himself has presented something utterly new and
wrought through him things never heard or seen before. . . . 3.
And what is newer than the marvel of imperial virtue given to the
human race by the wisdom of God. For he continues to be an

ambassador for the Christ of God with all boldness toward all persons, not hiding from the Savior's shame but speaking with reverence about the matter. He has declared himself openly, now signing, now priding himself on the trophy which led him to victory.

3.3.1. Besides this, he erected in front of the imperial palace for the eyes of all to see a painting on a very tall billboard, giving the Savior's sign inscribed above his head and depicting the enemy and savage adversary who has wasted the church of God through the tyranny of the ungodly, carried headlong into the abyss in the form of a dragon. For the oracles in the books of God's prophets have described him as a dragon and as a crooked serpent. 2. For this reason the emperor publicly displayed the dragon under his own and his children's feet, pierced with an arrow and plunging headlong into the depths of the sea. Here he was depicting the secret adversary of the human race and was wanting to make clear that he had been consigned to the abyss of destruction by the power of the Savior's trophy displayed over his head. 3. But this flower had been depicted with colors in the picture. I am awed by the intellectual greatness of this emperor. He depicted as if by divine inspiration what the voices of the prophets were crying out everywhere about this monster, saying that "God would bring his great and fearful sword upon the dragon, that crooked serpent, upon the dragon, the fleeing serpent, and would destroy the dragon in the sea" (Isa. 27:1). The emperor captured these things in images, truly representing this statement in a picture.

3.11. The first bishop on the right side got up and gave a measured speech, addressing the emperor and raising a hymn of thanksgiving to Almighty God for him. When he sat down again, all were silent as they fixed their gaze on the emperor. Looking on the hushed scene with bright eyes on all, he gathered together his thoughts and delivered the following speech in a quiet and gentle voice:

3.12.1. It was my prayerful goal, friends, to enjoy your harmonious gathering. Having obtained this, I give thanks to the universal Emperor because he has granted me the greatest good of all, I mean, not only to learn that you are all gathered together but to see one shared, harmonious sentiment among you all. 2. Let no malign enemy, therefore, mar our happy situation. Now that the tyrants' fight against God has been routed by the power of our Savior God, let none heap blasphemies on the divine law. In my mind internal strife within the church of God is worse than all war and horrible conflict, and they appear to me to be more grievous than those which go on outside the church. 3. Accordingly, when I achieved victories against my enemies by the will and assistance of God, I thought there was nothing left but to give thanks to God and to rejoice with those he liberated through us. But as soon as I learned with considerable surprise of your division, I did not cast the report aside but sent immediately to request your presence, hoping that I might supply some cure for this through my service. 4. Now I rejoice in seeing your assembly. But I judge that my prayers will have been fulfilled especially when I see all of you shouting in your souls and deciding on one common agreement of peace with all which it would be fitting for you who have consecrated yourselves to God to commend to others. Don't delay, then, friends, ministers of God and good servants of our common Lord and Savior. Begin now to bring out into the open the causes of this schism among you and to loosen every bond of controversy by pursuing the rules of peace. For if you acted in this manner you would do what is pleasing to God of all, and you would give abundant thanks to me, your fellow servant.

4.24. Thence it is fitting that he once, when receiving a group of bishops in his apartment, let the word slip out that he too was a bishop, when he said the following words in my hearing: "You have been appointed by God as a bishop of those who are inside the church, but I have been appointed by God as a bishop of those outside the church." And he truly adhered to his word, for he watched over all his subjects in a thoughtful way and exhorted them insofar as they could to live a godly life.

XXIV.

Corpus Permixtum

AUGUSTINE ON BAPTISM
BOOK 1

1.1. In the treatise which I wrote against the letter Parmenian devoted to Tyconius, I promised that I was going to treat the question of baptism more carefully. Even if I had not promised that there, I am not unmindful of the debt I owe to pleas of brothers and sisters. In this work, therefore, with the Lord's help I have undertaken not only to refute the objections which the Donatists usually raise against us about this matter, but also to present what the Lord has given us to say from the authority of the blessed martyr Cyprian, from whom they attempt to prop up their perversity lest it fall under the impact of truth. I am doing this so that all whose judgment is not blinded by eagerness to cause factions may understand not only that they are not helped by the authority of Cyprian but are rather refuted and overturned by it.

2. In the books mentioned above, it has already been said that baptism can be given outside the catholic communion just as it can also be retained outside it. None of the Donatists, however, deny that even the apostates have baptism, for it is not repeated in the case of those who return and are converted through penance, and no one concludes that they have lost it. So also those who leave the communion of the church through the sacrilege of schism certainly retain the baptism which they received before they left. For even if they depart, baptism is not administered to them again. From this it is proven that what they received when in a position of unity could not have been lost when they separated. For if it can be retained outside, why can't it be given there also? If you say, "It is not rightly given outside but yet is given,"

we respond: "Just as it is not rightly retained outside and yet is retained, so also it is not rightly given outside but yet is given." Just as what was possessed without benefit outside it begins to be beneficial by virtue of reconciliation to unity, so what was given without benefit outside it begins to be useful through the same reconciliation. Yet it is not right to say that what was given was not given, or to defame anyone by saying that person had not given this when a person confesses that he has given what he had himself received. For it is the sacrament of Baptism which the person who is baptized possesses, and it is the sacrament for administering Baptism which the person who is ordained possesses. But just as the baptized person does not lose the sacrament of Baptism if she should withdraw from unity, so too the ordained person does not lose the sacrament for administering Baptism if he should withdraw from unity. We must wrong neither sacrament. If one departs from evil persons, both depart; if one stays with evil persons, both stay. Therefore, just as we accept a baptism which one who should depart from unity cannot lose, so must we accept a baptism administered by a person who could not lose the sacrament for administering Baptism even though he should leave the church. For just as those who were baptized before they withdrew are not rebaptized when they return, so those who were ordained before they withdrew are not ordained again when they return. Either they perform the ministry they were performing, should the needs of the church demand that, or, if they do not perform a ministry, they at least perform the sacrament of their own ordination. Moreover, they are not placed among the laity when hands are laid on them. For Felicianus lost neither the sacrament of Baptism nor the sacrament for administering Baptism when he departed from them with Maximian. So now they have a person among themselves whom he baptized when he was outside in the Maximian schism. For this reason others could receive from them what they had not lost when they withdrew from our communion since they had not withdrawn to our communion. This shows that those who attempt to rebaptize persons in unity with the catholic church act impiously and that we who do not dare to reject the sacraments of God even when administered in schism itself act rightly. For in this they think the same as we do and also are with us, but in it they withdrew from us in what they dissented from us. This unity and disunity must not be measured by physical rather than spiritual motives. For just as bodies are united in joining of parts, so is there some contact of souls in agreement of wills. Therefore, if anyone who withdraws from unity wishes to do something other than what she perceives in unity, in that she pulls away and is detached. But where she accepts and learns what she wants to do as is done in unity, in that she remains attached and is united.

2.3. Therefore, they are with us in some things, but they have departed from us in some. Accordingly, we do not forbid them to do the things in which they are with us. But in things in which they are not with us, we urge them to come and accept them or return and receive them from us. In whatever ways we can, we do our loving best to see that they choose to emend and correct what is lacking. Consequently, we do not say to them, "Don't administer Baptism," but "Don't administer Baptism in schism." And we do not say to those whom they are going to baptize, "Don't receive Baptism," but "Don't receive Baptism in schism." For if extreme need should compel someone strongly where a person could not find a catholic through whom she may receive baptism and would receive what she was about to receive in the unity of the catholic church itself at the hands of someone outside the catholic unity, while preserving catholic peace in her mind, we would not think of her as anything but a catholic even if she should depart from this life immediately. But if she were freed by physical death after she had returned physically to a catholic congregation from which she had never departed in heart, not only do we not reprove what she did, but we praise it most surely and truly because she believed that God was present to her heart where she was keeping the unity of the church and was unwilling to depart this life without the Sacrament of Holy Baptism, which she knew is not of human but of divine origin wherever it is found. However, if anyone chooses by some perversity of mind to be baptized in schism when she could receive it in the catholic church itself, she is beyond question perverted and evil, doubly so because she knows what she is doing, even though she later decides to come to the catholic church because she is certain to benefit from the sacrament which she can receive elsewhere but cannot benefit from. For just as she does not doubt that what she receives elsewhere will benefit her in the catholic church, so she does not doubt that it is rightly to be received there.

3.4. We are saying two things, that there is baptism in the catholic church and that it is rightly received only there. The Donatists deny both of these. Likewise, we say two other things, that there is baptism among the Donatist but that it is not rightly received there. They vigorously affirm one of these, that is, that there is baptism there, but they won't admit that it is not rightly received there. Only three of these four statements are ours, but both of us agree on one. For we alone say that there is baptism in the catholic church and that it is rightly received there and that it is not rightly received among the Donatists. But that there is also baptism among the Donatists both they assert and we conceded. Suppose someone wants to be baptized and is already convinced that our church must be chosen to receive Christian salvation and that Christ's baptism is beneficial in it alone, even though it was received elsewhere. Yet he wants to be baptized still in the Donatist faction because not just they alone nor we alone but both of us agree that there is baptism there. This person should pay attention to the other three points. For if one chooses to follow us in the things they do not say but places the things which we both say before those which we alone say, it is enough for us if he places the things which they do not say and we alone say before those which they alone say. However, we assert that there is baptism in the catholic church, they do not. We assert that baptism is rightly received in the catholic church, they do not. We assert that baptism is not rightly received in the Donatists' faction, they do not. Therefore, just as a person believes rather what we alone say must be believed, so let that person do what we alone say must be done. But if he thinks so, let him believe more strongly what both of us say must be believed than what is said by us alone. For he is inclined to believe more strongly that Christ's baptism exists in the faction of Donatus because both of us agree than that baptism exists in the catholic church because this is said only by catholics. But again he is inclined to believe that Christ's baptism exists among us also because we alone say so than that it does not exist among us because they alone say so, for he has already determined and is convinced that we must be placed above them in things we disagree on. Therefore, he is inclined to believe that what we alone say is more rightly received among us than not rightly received because they alone say this. By the same rule he is more inclined to believe that baptism is not rightly received among them, as we alone say, than that it is rightly received, as they alone say. It seems somewhat foolish to him, therefore, to receive the baptism which we both agree is there but do not agree that it must be received there. So he chooses instead to unite with us in what we do not both agree on. Let him, therefore, receive baptism with confidence where it is sure both to be and to be received rightly, but let him not receive it where they indeed say it exists but do not say that it must be received from those whose thought he decided to opt for. Although he were not to have any doubt that he would receive in the Donatist church what he was sure he would receive rightly in the catholic church, he would make a terrible mistake to do this in regard to matters which pertain to the salvation of the soul or even in preferring uncertainty to certainty. At any rate it is sure that a person is to be baptized in the catholic church by the very fact that the person rightly baptized elsewhere even decided to come over to it. But let this person consider it at least uncertain whether a person is rightly baptized among the Donatists, since this is said by those whose thought he considers preferable to that of the Donatists. Since he prefers certainty to uncertainty, let him be baptized where he is quite sure it is done rightly because he decided he had to change to this church when he was thinking of being baptized in the other one.

4.5. But if anyone does not yet understand how it can happen that we say what we admit is there is not rightly administered there, let that person pay attention to our statement that it is not there rightly, just as they say in the case of those who leave their communion. Let her consider also the analogy of a military insignia that can be both possessed and received by deserters outside the army, but yet must neither be possessed nor received, and is neither changed nor renewed when a soldier is reenlisted or brought back to the army. Nevertheless, it is one thing for people to run unwisely to these heretics, thinking that the true church of Christ is there. But it is another thing for those who know that there is no other catholic church than the one which, just as has been promised, is spread throughout the world and extends to the ends of the earth. This church, growing among tares and longing for a rest some day from the weariness of scandals, says in the Psalms, "From the ends of the earth I have cried out to you, when my soul was weary. You have lifted me up onto a rock" (Ps. 61:2). But the rock was Christ, in whom the apostle says that we have been already raised from the dead and are sitting in heaven, though in hope rather than in actuality. Thus the Psalm goes on to say, "You have led me because you have become my hope, a tower of strength in the face of my enemy" (Ps. 61:2–3). From these promises, stored up like spears and javelins in a well-fortified fortress, the enemy is not only warned but also fought. He clothes his wolves in sheepskins so that they may say, "Lo, here is Christ. Lo, there!" (Matt. 24:23), and separate many from the catholicity of the city set on a hill to the factionalism of their own snares where they slaughter them. Although they know this, these persons choose to receive Christ's baptism outside the communion of the unity of the body of Christ, intending to change afterwards to the same communion with the baptism, knowing they are going to live in opposition to the church of Christ on the very day they receive it. If this is wicked, who is going to say, "Permit me to be wicked for just one day"? I ask why, if that person intends to change to the catholic church. What is he going to respond except that it is evil to be in the faction of Donatus and not to be in the unity of the catholic church? As many days as you do this evil, therefore, by that many days you are liable to do evil. It can be said that worse evil is done by more days and less by fewer, but it cannot be said that no evil is done. But what need is there to commit such an accursed evil for either one day or one hour? For a person who wants this kind of license to be given might as well seek a license to apostatize for a day either from the church or from God himself. For there is no reason why one should fear being an apostate for one day and not fear being a schismatic or heretic for one day.

5.6. "I prefer to receive Christ's baptism where both agree it is," this person says. But those whom you are about to join say that it is not received rightly here, while those from whom you are about to depart say that it is rightly received there. That is either false or, more mildly said, uncertain which is said by those persons whom you yourself regard as having less authority than those who speak against them, whom you yourself prefer. Therefore, put truth before falsehood or certainty before uncertainty. For not only those whom you are going to join but also you who are about to join confess that the thing you desire can be received rightly where you are about to join, even though you received it elsewhere. For if you should doubt whether it can be received rightly there, you should also doubt whether you should make the change. If it is uncertain whether it is a sin to receive baptism in the faction of Donatus; therefore, who can doubt that it is definitely a sin not to receive it where it is sure not to be a sin? But those who are baptized there through ignorance, thinking that it is the true church of Christ, surely sin less by comparison with them. Yet they do not escape serious injury from the sacrilege of schism, because others are more seriously hurt. For when it is said to some, "It will be more tolerable for Sodom in the day of judgment than for you" (Matt. 11:24), it does not mean that the Sodomites will not suffer torment, but that the others will suffer even more severely.

7. Nevertheless, this point was perhaps obscure and uncertain at times. But what becomes a source of healing for those who turn and are corrected is a burden to those who obstinately persist to their own ruin when they are no longer allowed to be ignorant. For the condemnation of the Maximianists and the restoration of those condemned along with those whom they baptized in the schism "in sacrilege outside their own communion" (to use the language of their own council), resolved this whole question and removed the whole controversy. It left no issue at all between us and the Donatists who communicate with Primianus, for it removed all doubt that Christ's baptism can not only be retained but also be given by those who are separated from the church. For just as they are compelled to acknowledge that those whom Felicianus baptized in schism had received true baptism (for they now have them in their constituency with that baptism which they received in schism), so we say that Christ's baptism also exists outside the catholic communion, which those who have cut themselves off from that communion give because they did not lose it when they were cut off. What they think they have conferred on those whom Felicianus baptized in schism when they reconciled them with themselves (that is, not that they

might receive what they did not have but that what they received and retained in schism without benefit might be beneficial to them), God really confers and bestows through the catholic communion upon those who come from some heresy or schism where they received Christ's baptism. In other words, they do not begin to have the sacrament of Baptism which they did not have before, but rather the sacrament which they had now begins to benefit them.

6.8. Therefore, there is no longer any controversy about this between us and those who are in some sense the chief Donatists, of whom Primianus is bishop in Carthage. For God wanted the controversy to be ended through the Maximianists so that they might agree by the force of his example to do what they would not do by the persuasion of love. But let us discuss this matter further lest those who do not communicate with the Primianists appear to have a good case when they contend that the Donatists have remained much more sincere the fewer there are of them. If these were Maximianists alone, we ought not to despise their claim to salvation. How much more, then, must we discuss this by virtue of the fact that this same party of Donatus has been split into many of the most minute factions. All of these minute factions reproach this much greater one in which Primianus is because they received baptism from Maximianists, and each of them tries to assert that the true baptism has remained among them alone and exists nowhere else, neither in the whole world where the catholic church reaches nor in the larger faction of Donatus nor among others of those very minute factions but only in itself. If all these factions would turn to the voice not of a human being but of the most evident truth itself and bridle the fiery spirit of their own perversity, they would return not merely to the larger faction of Donatus, from which fragment they have been cut, but from their own aridity to the very greenness of the catholic root. Certainly all those "who are not against us are for us, but when they do not gather with us, they scatter" (cf. Matt. 12:30).

7.9. The obscurity of this question in earlier days of the church before the Donatist schism forced great persons and even our fathers, the bishops, who are possessed of great love, to dispute and to vacillate so among themselves in preserving the peace of the church that for a long time the different statutes of councils held in their particular areas varied a lot. Finally, what was thought to be most wholesome was established by a plenary council of the whole world, all doubts removed. Lest I seem to base my case on purely human arguments, therefore, I bring forth from the gospel clear proofs by which, the Lord helping, I show how rightly and truly God would like for the church's medicine to cure that wound by which any schismatic or heretic is separated from the church. But whatever remained healthy should be approved when recognized rather than wounded by disapproval. It is true that the Lord says in the Gospel, "Whoever is not with me is against me, and whoever does not gather with me scatters" (Matt. 12:30). Yet when the disciples had reported to him that they had seen some casting out demons in his name and had forbidden it because they were not among his followers, he says, "Don't forbid it. Whoever is not against us is for us. For no one can do anything in my name and speak badly about me" (Mark 9:38–39). If there was nothing in that person to be corrected, then anyone who gathers in the name of Christ, having established himself outside the communion of the church and dissociating himself from Christian society, would be safe. And thus the statement would be false that "Whoever is not with me is against me, and whoever does not gather with me scatters." But if he is to be corrected in what the Lord said, as the disciples of the Lord wanted to do through ignorance, why did he forbid that to be forbidden, "Don't forbid it." And how will what he says here be true, "Whoever is not against you is for you"? For in this deed he was not against them but for them where he was healing through Christ's name. What must we understand so that both of these statements may be true, as they are, namely, "Whoever is not with me is against me, and whoever does not gather with me scatters" and also "Don't forbid it, for whoever is not against you is for you"? We must understand nothing else than that this person was to be affirmed in his veneration of such a great name where he was not against the church but for it and yet to be blamed in that separation where he scattered when he gathered. Therefore, if he should come by chance to the church he would not receive what he already possessed but would be corrected where he had erred.

8.10. For the prayers of the Gentile Cornelius did not go

unheard nor his alms unaccepted. On the contrary, he was counted worthy both for the angel to be sent to him and to see the messenger through whom he could learn everything he needed to know without access to any human agency. But because none of the good he possessed in his prayers and almsgiving could benefit him unless he was incorporated into the church by the bond of Christian society and peace, he was ordered to send to Peter and learn about Christ through him. After being baptized by him, he was also joined in communion with the society of Christian people, with whom he had previously been joined only by the similarity of good deeds. It would certainly have been ruinous to have despised good he did not yet possess, being boastful on the basis of what he had. So also if those who separate themselves from the society of others and burst the bond of unity, doing violence to love, do none of the things which they received in that society, they are separated in all things. Therefore, if anyone whom they associated with should want to come to the church, that person ought to receive everything she has not yet received. But if they do some of the same things, they have not separated themselves in those and they are retained by that part in the framework of the church. In other things they are cut off. Hence, if anyone whom they associated with is connected to the church by that part in which they have not been separated and should want to come to the church, she is healed at the point where she was torn and erred. But where she was well and connected with the church, she is not cured but recognized, lest we inflict a greater wound by wanting to cure what is well. Those whom the Donatists baptize, therefore, are healed from the wound of idolatry or unbelief, but they hurt them still more with the wound of schism. For among the people of God a sword killed idolaters, but a hole in the ground swallowed schismatics. The apostle says, "If I have all faith so as to move mountains but do not have love, I am nothing" (1 Cor. 13:2).

11. Suppose someone is brought to the doctor afflicted with a grave wound in one of the vital parts of the body. If the doctor should say, "He is going to die unless it is cured," I don't think those who brought him would be so foolish as to examine and count the other healthy members of his body and then respond to the doctor, "Can it be that all these healthy members can't keep

him alive and this one diseased organ cause his death?" Surely they do not say this. Rather, they simply bring the person to be cured. Moreover, they do not ask when they bring him that the doctor cure the healthy members also, but that he apply medicine immediately to that one spot where death threatens the other healthy parts as well and will occur unless it is healed. What does it benefit a person, then, to have either sound faith or perhaps only a sound sacrament of faith when the soundness of love is destroyed by the fatal wound of schism, with the result that these sound elements are also dragged toward death by its destruction? Lest that happen, the mercy of God through the unity of the holy church never ceases so that they may come and be cured by the medicine of reconciliation through the bond of peace. Let them not think that they are sound because we say they have something which is sound. On the other hand, let them not think that what is sound must be cured again because we show that something is wounded. In the soundness of the sacrament, therefore, because they are not against us, they are for us; but in the wound of schism whatever they do not gather with Christ, they scatter. Why do they pass proud eyes over what is sound? Let them humbly condescend to look at their wound and pay attention not only to what is there but also to what is not there.

9.12. Let them see how many and what great things are of no benefit if one thing is lacking. And let them see what that one thing is. Let them not hear me but the apostle on this point: "If I speak with tongues of men and angels," he says, "but do not have love, I have become a noisy gong and a clanging cymbal. And if I have the gift of prophecy and know all mysteries and all knowledge, and if I have all faith so as to move mountains, but do not have love, I am nothing" (1 Cor. 13:1–2). What benefit is it to them, then, if they have both angelic speech in the sacred mysteries and the gift of prophecy, like Caiaphas and Saul, so that they may sometimes prophesy, when Holy Scripture attests that they were liable to be condemned? Or if they not only know but also have the mysteries, as Simon Magus had? Or if they had confessed faith, like the demons confessed Christ (for they were not unbelieving when they said, "What is there between us and you, Son of God? We know who you are.")? Or if they have even distributed their possessions among the poor, as many do not only in the catholic church but in various heresies? Or if they deliver their own body to the flames along with us in some violent persecution for the faith which they confess equally with us? Yet because they do these things separated from the church, not "bearing up with one another in love" nor "being eager to keep the unity of the Spirit in the bond of peace," because they do not have love, they cannot attain to eternal salvation, even with all those things which are of no benefit to them.

10.13. But they think they are very clever when they ask whether Christ's baptism begets children in the Donatist party or not. If we concede that it does, then they may claim that their church is the mother who can beget children from the baptism of Christ. And since there must be one church, they may then charge that ours is not the church. But if we say, "It does not beget children," they say, "Why then are those who switch from us to you not reborn by baptism, when they were baptized among us, if they have not yet been born?"

14. But this is to argue as if it begets children from that in which it is separated and not from that in which it is connected. For it is separated from the bond of love and peace, but it is connected in one baptism. Therefore, there is one church which alone is called catholic. Whatever this church has in different communions separated from its unity, she and not they beget children by virtue of that which she has of her own in them. For their separation does not beget children but what they retained from her. If they lose this, they do not beget children at all. She whose sacraments are retained, therefore, bears children in all communions. Consequently such offspring can be begotten anywhere, although not all whom she begets belong to her unity, which will save those who persevere to the end. For it is not only those who have been manifested by the open sacrilege of separation who do not belong to her, but also those who are separated by evil life, though joined corporately to her unity. For the church herself had given birth to Simon Magus through baptism. Yet he was told that he would have no part in the inheritance of Christ. Did he lack anything in baptism, the gospel, or the sacraments? No. It was because he lacked love that he was born in vain, and perhaps it would have been better had he never been born. Were they not born to whom the apostle says, "As babes in Christ, I gave you

milk to drink, not meat" (1 Cor. 3:1–2)? Yet he recalls them from the sacrilege of schism into which they were rushing because they were carnal. "As babes in Christ," he says, "I gave you milk to drink, not meat, for you were not yet able to eat it. But you are still not able, for you are still carnal. When there are envy and strife among you, are you not carnal and do you not walk in a purely human manner? For when one says, 'I am Paul's,' but another, 'I am Apollo's,' are you not purely human?" (1 Cor. 3:1–4). For he says about these above, "I beg you, brothers and sisters, by the name of our Lord Jesus Christ that you all say the same thing and that there be no schisms among you. Rather, be perfected in the same mind and in the same understanding. For it has been reported to me, my brothers and sisters, by Chloe's group, that there are contentions among you. I mean this, that each of you is saying, 'I am Paul's, I am Apollo's, I am Cephas's, I am Christ's.' Has Christ been divided? Paul was not crucified for you, was he? Or you weren't baptized into Paul's name, were you?" (1 Cor. 1:10–13). If these continued in this obstinacy and perversity, therefore, certainly they were born; but they would not belong by the bond of peace and unity to that very church from which they were born. Therefore, she herself begets them both through her own womb and through the wombs of her handmaidens from the same sacraments, as it were, from the seed of her husband. For it was not in vain that the apostle says that all things were done figuratively. But the proud are not united with their lawful mother. They are like Ishmael, about whom it is said, "Cast out the handmaiden and her son, for the son of the handmaiden will not be an heir along with my son Isaac" (Gen. 21:10). But those who love peaceably the lawful wife of their father and have been begotten by lawful succession are like the sons of Jacob even though born of handmaidens but yet receiving the same inheritance. But those who are born within the unity of the womb of the same mother and yet neglect the grace which they received are like Esau, the son of Isaac, who was rejected, as God attests, saying, "I loved Jacob, but I hated Esau" (Mal. 1:2–3; cf. Gen. 25:24), though both were conceived from one copulation and born from one womb.

11.15. They also ask whether sins are forgiven through baptism in the Donatist faction. If we say they are forgiven, they answer, "Therefore, the Holy Spirit is there because when it was given to the disciples as the Lord breathed on them, he then added, 'Baptize the nations in the name of the Father and of the Son and of the Holy Spirit. Whoever's sins you forgive, they will be forgiven that person; whoever's you retain, they will be retained' (Matt. 28:19; John 20:23). And if this is so," they say, "then our communion is the church of Christ. For the Holy Spirit does not effect forgiveness of sins beyond the church. And if our communion is the church of Christ, then your communion is not the church of Christ. For there is only one, whatever she is, about which it is said, 'My dove is one. She is her mother's only one' (Song of Sol. 6:8). There cannot be as many churches as there are schisms." But if we say that sins are not forgiven there, they say, "Therefore, there is no true baptism there, and you ought for that reason to baptize those whom you receive from us. Because you do not do that, you admit that you are not in the church of Christ."

16.   We reply to them according to the Scriptures, asking them to respond themselves to the questions they ask of us. I ask them to tell me whether sins are forgiven where there is no love. For sins are the darkness of the soul. Surely we hear John saying, "Whoever hates his brother is still in darkness" (1 John 2:11). But none could create schisms if they were not blinded by hatred of brothers and sisters. If, therefore, we say that sins are not forgiven there, how is a person who is baptized among them reborn? For what does it mean to be reborn through baptism except to be renewed from oldness? But how is anyone renewed from oldness whose past sins are not forgiven? If one is not reborn, that person does not put on Christ. From this it would seem to follow that this person must be baptized again, for the apostle says, "for inasmuch as you have been baptized in Christ, you have put on Christ" (Gal. 3:27). If he has not put him on, then he should not be considered to have been baptized in Christ. Further, since we say "baptized in Christ," we confess that a person has "put on Christ." And if we confess this, we confess that that person has been reborn. If that is true, then sins have also been forgiven. If forgiveness of sins has not happened already, then why does John say, "Whoever hates his brother or sister still abides in darkness" (1 John 2:11)? Or is there no hatred of brothers and sisters in

schism? Who would say this when the beginning and the continuance of schism is nothing but hatred of brothers and sisters?

17. They appear to give an answer to this question when they say, "Therefore, there is no forgiveness of sins in schism and for that reason no recreation of the new humanity or even baptism of Christ." But since we admit that Christ's baptism exists there, we propose that they solve the question whether Simon Magus was baptized with the true baptism of Christ. They will answer "yes," for they are forced to do so by the authority of the Holy Scripture. I ask, then, whether they admit that his sins were forgiven. They will certainly admit it. Next, I ask why Peter said that he had no part in the lot of the saints. "Because he sinned afterwards," they say, "wanting to buy the gift of God with money. He believed the apostles were vendors of this gift."

12.18. Why? If he approached his baptism deceitfully, were his sins forgiven or not? Let them choose what they wish. Whichever they choose is all we need. Should they say that they were not forgiven, I ask whether it would be decided that he should be baptized again if he later confessed his deception with remorseful heart and genuine grief. If it is pure folly to say this, let them admit that a person can be baptized with the true baptism of Christ and yet his heart not allow abolition of sins to happen because it persists in malice or sacrilege. Thus let them understand that people can be baptized in communions separated from the church where Christ's baptism is given and received with the same celebration of the sacrament. Nevertheless, this baptism only becomes beneficial for forgiveness of sins when the person is reconciled to the unity of the church and purged of the sacrilege of discord in which his sins were retained and not allowed to be forgiven. For just as happened in the case of the one who approached baptism deceitfully, he is not baptized again but is cleansed by pious correction and truthful confession (which would not be possible without baptism) so that the baptism administered before might begin then to be beneficial when that deception withdraws in the face of the truthful confession. So also that person who received Christ's baptism which those who separated themselves did not lose while an enemy of the love and the peace of Christ in some heresy or schism, a wicked sacrilege in which his sins were not forgiven. When he corrected himself and came to the society and unity of the church, he should not be baptized again, because he shows by that very reconciliation and peace that he is beginning in unity to have the benefit for forgiveness of sins of the sacrament which was not beneficial when received in schism.

19. But suppose they should say in the case of the one who approached deceitfully that his sins were forgiven at that point in time by the holy power of such a great sacrament but that they returned immediately because of his deception. Thus the Holy Spirit would both be present with the person baptized so that sins might withdraw and also flee before the continuance of the deception so that the sins might return. This would confirm both the statement, "As many of you as have been baptized in Christ, you have put on Christ," and also, "For the Holy Spirit of discipline will flee deception" (Gal. 3:27; Wisd. of Sol. 1:5). In other words, the sanctity of baptism clothes a person in Christ, and the continuance of deception strips him of Christ, as happens when anyone passes from darkness through the light to darkness. That person's eyes are directed perpetually toward the darkness, but the light is not able to shine upon him unless it passes through the darkness. If, then, they should say this, let them understand that this happens also in the case of those who are baptized outside the communion of the church but with the church's baptism. Baptism is holy wherever it may be by itself, and therefore it does not belong to those who separate themselves but to the church from which they separated. Nevertheless, it is beneficial even among them insofar as they pass through its light to the darkness of their discord. The sins which the sanctity of baptism forgave at that point in time return immediately, however, just as the darkness which the light had dispelled as they were passing through returns.

20. The Lord teaches quite plainly in the gospel that sins which have been forgiven can return when there is no love for brothers and sisters in the parable of that servant whom he forgave everything when he begged for it although he had found him owing ten thousand talents. But when this servant was not merciful to his fellow servant who owed him a hundred denarii, the lord ordered him to repay what he had forgiven him. The time at which a pardon is received through baptism is, as it were, a time of reckoning

so that all debts which have been found might be forgiven. Yet that servant did not later loan his fellow servant the money which he so pitilessly demanded when the latter could not pay, but his fellow servant already owed him when he gave an accounting to his lord and was freed from such a huge indebtedness. He did not forgive his fellow servant what he owed him and then approached his lord to be forgiven. The words of the fellow servant show this, "Be patient with me and I will repay you" (Matt. 18:26). Otherwise he would have said, "You forgave me this before. Why do you demand it again?" The words of the Lord himself disclose this more clearly, for he says, "But that servant went out and found one of his fellow servants who owed him a hundred denarii" (Matt. 18:26). He did not say, "Whose hundred denarii debt he had already forgiven." For if he had forgiven it, he would not still owe him. Therefore, because he said "he owed him," it is evident that he had not forgiven it. It would have been better certainly and more suitable for a debtor about to render an account for such a great debt and to hope for mercy from his lord that he should first forgive his fellow servant what he owed and thus approach his lord to render an account where the mercy of the lord must be implored. But the fact that he had not yet forgiven his fellow servant did not prevent his lord from forgiving him everything he owed at the time he was receiving an accounting. But what did it benefit him since all his debts were again immediately turned back on his head on account of the persistence of his hatreds. So the grace of baptism is not prevented from forgiving all sins, although hatred of brothers and sisters persists in the mind of one to whom they are forgiven. For the sins of yesterday and whatever was before that are forgiven, even at the very hour and moment before baptism and in baptism. But thereafter one begins to be liable immediately not only for the following but also for the past days, hours, moments. All sins which have been forgiven may return. And often these affect persons in the church.

13.21. For it often happens that a person has an enemy whom she hates unfairly, even though we are commanded to love even our enemies and to pray for them. But in immediate danger of death she begins to be upset and asks for baptism which she receives in such haste that the time of danger scarcely allows the required examination of a few words, much less of the very long conversation which would be required to drive this hatred from the heart, even if it should be known by the one baptizing her. Certainly cases like this do not cease to come out not only among us but also among them. What, then do we say? Are the sins of this person forgiven or not? Let them choose just which one they want. For if they are forgiven, they return immediately. The gospel says it, the truth shouts it. Whether they are forgiven or not, therefore, medicine is needed afterwards. Yet if this person lives and learns that this must be corrected and corrects it, she is not baptized again either among them or among us. Thus also we do not correct the things which schismatics or heretics hold or do in ways other than the true church when they come to us. Rather, we approve them. For they are not separated from us in what they do not differ from us. Nevertheless, because these things are of no benefit to them so long as they are schismatics or heretics, on account of the other things in which they differ from the truth and on account of the very monstrous evil of their separation itself, whether their sins remain in them or return immediately after being forgiven, we urge them to come to the safety of peace and love, not only that they may obtain something they did not have but that what they have may begin to be of some benefit to them.

14.22. It is useless, therefore, for them to say, "If you accept our baptism, what are we lacking which makes you think we ought to join your communion?" For we respond: It is not your baptism which we accept, because baptism is not the baptism of schismatics or heretics but of God and of the church, wherever it may be found and however brought there. You have nothing but depraved thought and sacrilegious deed and impious separation. For you would lack one thing, if everything else was true which you either had or thought, and you still persist in the same separation against the bond of fraternal peace against the unity of all brothers and sisters who have been displayed throughout the world just as promised. You could never in any way examine the cases of all these people and know their hearts so as to have a right to condemn them. Moreover, they cannot be blamed because they entrusted their cases to the judges of the church rather than to accusers. You lack this one thing—what a person lacks who does not have love. What need is there to go back over the same ground? Look in the apostle and see for yourselves how much it is you are lacking. But what does it matter to one who does not have love whether he is blown away outside by some wind of temptation or stays within the Lord's harvest to be separated at the last winnowing? Yet even such persons as these do not have to be born again if they have been born once in baptism.

15.23. Certainly the church gives birth to all through baptism, either in herself, that is, from her own womb, or outside herself, from her husband's seed. Esau, on the one hand, though born of a wife rather than a handmaiden, was separated from the people of God on account of fraternal discord. Asher, on the other hand, born it is true by the authorization of a wife but of a handmaiden, attained the promised land on account of fraternal concord. Whence also in the case of Ishmael, it was not the fact that his mother was a handmaiden but fraternal discord which led to his separation from the people of God. He did not benefit from the power of the wife whose son he was because it was by her own conjugal rights that he was conceived in and born of the handmaiden. In the same way is the case of the Donatists. Whoever are born are born by right of the church which is in baptism. If they agree with brothers and sisters, they will enter the promised land through the unity of peace, not being ejected again from their mother's womb but being recognized in the semen of their father. But if they persist in discord, they will belong to the line of Ishmael. Ishmael was first, Isaac second. Esau was first, but Jacob later. This does not mean that heresy gives birth before the church or that the church gives birth first to the carnal and natural and then to the spiritual, but that in the lot of our mortality itself by which we are born of Adam, "what is spiritual is not first but what is natural, afterward what is spiritual" (1 Cor. 15:46). But because "the natural person does not perceive what is of the Spirit of God" (1 Cor. 2:14), all dissensions and schisms are begotten by this "natural" mentality. The apostle says that those who persist in this mentality belong to the old covenant, that is, to the desire for earthly promises in which spiritual things certainly are modeled, but "the natural person does not perceive what is of the Spirit of God."

24. Whenever human beings begin in this life to be the kind of

persons who, though touched by the divine mysteries appointed for distribution in this world, savor carnal things anyway and hope and desire carnal things both in this life and after this life, they are "natural." But the church, which is the people of God, is an ancient thing on pilgrimage in this life, having a "natural" share in some persons, a spiritual in others. The old covenant belongs to the "natural," the new to the "spiritual." But in the earliest times both were hidden from Adam to Moses. But the old covenant was made manifest by Moses and the new was hidden in it, because it was signified in a secret way. But after the Lord came in the flesh, the new was revealed. The mysteries of the old ceased, but such desires did not cease. For they are in those whom the apostle still calls "natural," even though they have already been born through the mystery of the new covenant, since they are incapable of perceiving what is of the Spirit of God. For just as some used to live as "spiritual" persons on the sacraments of the old covenant, belonging secretly of course to the new covenant which was then hidden, so also now many live as "natural" persons on the sacrament of the new covenant which has now been revealed. If these don't progress so as to perceive what is of the Spirit of God, as the apostolic word urges them, they will still belong to the old covenant. But if they make progress, by that very progression and approach they belong to the new even before they lay hold on them. If they are snatched from this life before they become spiritual, protected by the sanctity of the sacrament, they are considered to be in the land of the living where our hope is and where the Lord is our portion. I find no truer interpretation of the Scripture, "Your eyes have seen me in my imperfection" (Ps. 139:16), than in what follows, "And all will be inscribed in your book."

16.25. But the woman who begot Abel and Enoch and Noah and Abraham also begot Moses and the later prophets before the advent of the Lord. And the woman who begot those also begot the apostles and our martyrs and all good Christians. For although all appeared to have been born at different times, they belong to the society of a single people and, as citizens of the same state, they have experienced them and others will experience them until the end. Likewise, the same woman who begot Cain and Ham and Ishmael and Esau also begot Dathan and others like him in the same people. And the same woman who begot those also begot Judas, the false apostle, and Simon Magus and other pseudo–Christians who up to this day have obstinately persisted in natural affection, whether they have been mixed into the unity of the church or separate from it in open schism. But when such persons have the gospel preached to them by those who are spiritual and are touched by the sacraments, Rebecca as it were gives birth to them by herself as she gave birth to Esau. But when such persons are begotten in the people of God by those who do not proclaim the gospel purely, Sarah indeed gives birth to them but through Hagar. Likewise, when the spiritually good are begotten by the preaching or baptizing of carnal persons, it is Leah and Rachel who give birth to them by conjugal right but through the womb of a handmaiden. But when good and faithful persons are begotten in the gospel through spiritual persons and either move toward an attitude of spiritual maturity or do not cease to strive in that direction or at least do not do so only because they can't, they are born to a new life and the new covenant like Isaac was born from the womb of Sarah or Jacob from the womb of Rebecca.

17.26. Therefore, whether they seem to dwell within or are openly outside, whatever is flesh is flesh. Whether they stay on the threshing floor in their barrenness or are blown outside as if by the wind when temptation occurs, what is straw is straw. Even the person who mixes with the congregation of the saints in carnal obstinacy is separated from the unity of that church which is "without spot or wrinkle." Yet we must not despair of anyone, whether such a person appears within or lives more openly outside. But the spiritual, or those who are progressing toward this goal with pious eagerness, do not go outside, for even when they seem to be expelled by some perversity or human necessity, they show themselves more approved there than if they remain within, since they in no way rise up against the church but are based in the strongest foundation of love upon the solid rock of unity. Pertinent to this is what is said in the sacrifice of Abraham, "But he did not cut the birds in two" (Gen. 15:20).

18.27. I think I have spent enough time, then, arguing about the question of baptism. Because this is quite clearly a schism which is called by the name of the Donatists, we have only to

111

believe devoutly about baptism what the universal church maintains apart from the sacrilege of schism. Yet if in the church some think one thing, others another about this question while keeping peace, until a universal council should affirm one clear and genuine position, love of unity should cover up the error of human weakness, as Scripture says, "For love covers up a multitude of sins" (1 Pet. 4:8.). For as other things do no good when love is absent, some do no harm when it is present.

28. There are great proofs of this in the letters of the blessed martyr Cyprian, if I may now come to him whose authority they carnally flatter themselves to possess, although spiritually they are overthrown by his love. For in his days, before the consensus of the whole church confirmed by the decree of a plenary council what must be observed in this matter, it seemed to him and about eighty fellow bishops of African churches that any person who had been baptized outside the communion of the catholic church ought to be baptized again when that person came into the church. I suppose the Lord did not reveal to such a great person that this was not the right thing to do so that his piety and humility and love in preserving the peace of the church in a healthy way might become evident and be noticed as an example of healing, so to speak, not only for Christians of that time but even later. For when a bishop of such merit, of such a church, of such a heart, of such eloquence, of such virtue should entertain an opinion about baptism other than the truth was going to affirm after more diligent inquiry (although many of his colleagues held what was not yet made quite clear but was sanctioned by the past custom of the church and afterwards embraced by the whole catholic world), he did not sever himself from others who thought differently by forming a separate communion. And he did not cease to persuade others also to "put up with one another in love, being eager to keep the unity of the spirit in the bond of peace" (cf. Eph. 4:2–3). For if any infirmity were found in some members, so long as the structure of the body remained, it might regain its health by their overall soundness more readily than it would if an effort to cure the disease was prevented by cutting it off of the body. If Cyprian had separated himself, how many would have followed! What a name he would have made for himself among humankind! How much more widely would the name Cyprianist be spread than

Donatist! But he was not a "son of perdition." It has been said about this sort, "You have hurled them down while they were lifted up" (cf. Ps. 73:18). But he was a son of the peace of the church who, though possessed of so much illumination of heart, did not see one thing so that another might be seen better through him. "And I will show you a still better way," says the apostle. "If I speak with the tongues of human beings and angels but do not have love, I have become a noisy gong or a clanging cymbal" (1 Cor. 12:31—13.1). Cyprian did not go too far, therefore, so that he might discern the secret mystery of the sacrament. But if he had known all mysteries but did not have love, it would have been nothing. But since he, with imperfect insight, preserved this humbly, faithfully, and bravely, he deserved to attain a martyr's crown. Consequently, if any cloud crept into his clear mind from the human condition, it would be dispelled by the glorious brightness of his gleaming blood. For it was not in vain that the Lord Jesus himself, when he called himself the vine but his own disciples branches on the vine, said that branches which did not bear fruit were to be cut off and taken away from the vine as useless. But who is the fruit unless it is that new offspring about whom he also says, "I give you a new commandment, that you love one another" (John 13:34)? This is that love without which other things are of no benefit. The apostle also says, "But the fruit of the Spirit is love, joy, peace, patience, kindness, goodness, faith, gentleness, self-control" (Gal. 5:22–23). All of these come from love and together make as it were a wonderful cluster. Yet it is not in vain that the Lord also added, "But whatever branches bear fruit in me, my father prunes them so that they may bring forth more fruit" (John 15:2). He would not have said this unless it was because those who are strong in the fruit of love may still have something to be purged which the farmer does not leave untended. Because this holy man, therefore, though holding a view of baptism which differed from the truth of the matter which afterwards was thoroughly examined and confirmed by the most careful examination, remained in the unity of the catholic church, he was repaid for the abundance of his charity and purified by the pruning hook of his martyrdom.

18.29. But lest I seem to speak these things in praise of the most blessed martyr (which certainly is not his but that of the

One he showed he was such a person) to avoid proving the case, let us now bring forward from his letters the proofs by which the mouths of the Donatists may especially be stopped. For they hurl his authority at the inexperienced so that they may prove they are doing what is right when they rebaptize believers who come to them. What wretches they are! Utterly damned unless they correct themselves—by themselves! They choose to imitate in such a great man the very thing which did not hurt him because he walked in persistent steps to the very end in that peace from which they have erred "who did not know the way of peace." It is true that Christ's baptism is holy everywhere. Although it may be among heretics or schismatics, it does not belong to the heresy or schism itself. Therefore, when they come to the catholic church from there, it is not necessary to rebaptize them. Nevertheless, rebaptism is one thing. It is another thing for those who stray from the catholic peace and have fallen into the evil pit of schism to decide that others must be baptized again. For the cluster of love covers up that speck on the brightness of a holy soul. But an implacable countenance shows this blackness in their hellish foulness. But since we are about to treat from this point on matters which relate to the authority of the blessed Cyprian, let us make a new start.

Bibliography

PRIMARY SOURCES

The Apostolic Fathers (*1 Clement*, *Didache*, Ignatius, *2 Clement*, *Martyrdom of Polycarp*, *Epistle to Diognetus*), ed. Kirsopp Lake. Loeb Classical Library. Cambridge: Harvard University Press; London: William Heinemann, 1959.

Augustine. *On Baptism: Against the Donatists*, ed. M. Petschenig. Corpus scriptorum ecclesiasticorum latinorum 51–53. Vienna: F. Tempsky, 1908–10.

Clement of Alexandria. *Exhortation to the Greeks, The Instructor, Miscellanies*, ed. Otto Stahlin. Die griechischen christlichen Schriftsteller der ersten drei Jahrhunderte 15, 17, 39. Leipzig: J. C. Hinrichs, 1905–36.

Cyprian. *On the Unity of the Church*, ed. E. H. Blakeney. New York: Macmillan Co.; London: S.P.C.K., 1928.

Eusebius. *The Life of Constantine*, ed. I. A. Heikel Die griechischen christlichen Schriftsteller der ersten drei Jahrhunderte 7. Leipzig: J. C. Hinrichs, 1902.

Irenaeus. *Against Heresies*, 2 vols., ed. W. Wigan Harvey. Cambridge: Cambridge University Press, 1857.

Justin. *Dialogue with Trypho*, ed. J. C. M. van Winden. Leiden: E. J. Brill, 1971.

_____. *Works*, 3d. ed., ed. J. C. Th. Otto. Jena: Hermann Dufft, 1876–81.

Origen. *Against Celsus, On Prayer*, ed. Paul Koetschau. Die griechischen christlichen Schriftsteller der ersten drei Jahrhunderte 2, 3. Leipzig: J.C. Hinrichs, 1899.

Pliny. *Letters*, rev. ed., ed. W. M. L. Hutchinson and William Melmoth. Loeb Classical Library. New York: Macmillan Co.; London: William Heinemann, 1915.

SECONDARY WORKS

Bardy, Gustave. *La théologie de l'église de saint Irénée au concile de Nicée.* Paris: Éditions du Cerf, 1947.

Benko, Stephen. *The Meaning of Sanctorum Communio.* Studies in Historical Theology 3. London: SCM Press, 1964.

Butler, B. C. *The Idea of the Church.* Baltimore: Helicon Press; London: Darton, Longman & Todd, 1962.

Campenhausen, Hans von. *Ecclesiastical Authority and Spiritual Power in the Church of the First Three Centuries,* trans. J. A. Baker. London: A. & C. Black, 1969.

Frend, W. H. C. *The Donatist Church: A Movement of Protest in Roman North Africa.* Oxford: Clarendon Press, 1952.

Greenslade, S. L. *Schism in the Early Church,* 2d ed. London: SCM Press, 1964.

Harnack, Adolf. *The Constitution and Law of the Church in the First Two Centuries,* trans. F. L. Pogson. ed. H. D. A. Major. New York: G. P. Putnam's Sons; London: Williams & Norgate, 1910.

Kelly, J. N. D. *Early Christian Doctrines,* 5th ed., chaps. 9, 15, 16. San Francisco: Harper & Row, 1978.

Rahner, Hugo. *Symbole der Kirche: Die Ekklesiologie der Väter.* Salzburg: Otto Müller Verlag, 1964.

Streeter, B. H. *The Primitive Church.* London: Macmillan & Co., 1929.